A MULTICULTURAL AMERICA

A MULTICULTURAL AMERICA

A Light For The World

John E. Valdez

SANTARROSA
PUBLISHING HOUSE

OCEANSIDE, CALIFORNIA

Published by Santarrosa Publishing House
Dedicated to supporting early-career authors and improving the quality of books published.
www.SantarrosaPublishingHouse.com

Written by John E. Valdez
Editing Assistance by Linda Rockafellow, Hal Lingerman
Overall Book Layout and Design by Ana Patiño
Cover Image by Andrew Howe. [Modified] E Pluribus Unum - Out of Many - One Seal of the United States, Getty Images Signature. Retrieved from Canva.com
Cover Design by Ana Patiño

Library of Congress Control Number: 2025909693
ISBN: 978-1-960589-00-2 (softcover)
ISBN: 978-1-960589-01-9 (hardcover)

Printed in the United States of America

ACKNOWLEDGEMENTS

In gratitude to my father, Eduardo Valdez, and mother, Justina Valdez Garcia. To my sister, Rose Duenez and brother, Carlos Valdez. To my son Joaquin "Kino" and daughter-in-law, Jessica Valdez Condon-Mann. To my daughter Micaela "Mica" Valdez. My grandchildren, Julian, Jordin and Jayden Valdez. My grandniece, Christine and husband Jason. My great, great grandnieces, Justice and Aidan Eldridge. My nephew Jack "Jackie" Ramirez. Nephew Steve Dueñez, partner Michelle and God-daughter Juliet Willis. Friends: Edgar and Norma Olivares, Pastor Bruce and Claudia De Soto.

Mentors, Archbishop John Raphael Quinn, Father William Shipley, professor of Philosophy and Dr. Ray Brandes, professor of History from the University of San Diego (USD). Dr. Carlos Blanco Aguinaga, professor of Spanish Literature at University of California at San Diego, La Jolla and Idis Blanco, renowned teacher of Anthropology and wife. Retired teacher from Pennsylvania, Cecilia Hord. Dr. Brophy from Helix High School, inspired teacher of English. Dr. Conrad, professor of Literature at USD devoted to the writings and philosophy of David Henry Thoreau. To my outstanding Phi Kappa Theta fraternity brothers from USD, you are amazing. Dr. Julian Nava professor and mentor former Ambassador to Mexico under President Jimmy Carter. Dr. Pat Drinan professor of International Relations and Dean of Arts and Sciences at USD. Dr. Marianne Drinan professor of Political Science at Palomar College.

In appreciation to Movimiento Estudiantil Chicano de Aztlán (MEChA) leaders Rolando Moreno, Dr. Luz Elena Garzon, Dr. Daniel Fikenthal, Dr. Rodolfo "Rudy" Jacobo, Henry Lesperance, Ethnic Studies professor, and PhD candidate at Claremont Graduate University in Cultural Studies. Special thanks to Palomar College mentors: Dr. Theodore Kilman, Vice President and Dean at Palomar College, Dean Gene Jackson, and Professor Bill Bedford, inspired leader, colleague and mentor, who encouraged me in my beginning years as a college instructor at Palomar College. To Kirk Whisler who introduced me to great authors, writers and publishers of Latino Literature and wonderful book festivals. In gratitude to Ana M. Patiño, my former student in Chicano history class who is working meticulously on my book layout and design, and who has prepared my book in numerous and wonderful ways. To my wonderful good friend and colleague, Reverend Hal

Lingerman, a brilliant and gifted writer and professor of creative writing and instructor of World Religions at Palomar College. His suggestions and revisions have helped me tremendously. I am very grateful for his reading and powerful and insightful comments. Maribel Castro-Morales, assistance in revision typing.

I am greatly blessed by St. Mary's Deacon Jim Kostick and wife, Carol Kostick, who have prayed for me and my family. I am ever grateful for their friendship, love and heartfelt daily prayers. With appreciation to St. Mary's Rosary Society prayer group of the twelve o'clock mass and Holy Rosary leader, Jan Bissi, Dr. Susan T. Feraris and all Holy Rosary participants. Divine Mercy Cenacle leader Jeanette Moser, Liz Westwood, and members. Gary, Jennifer, and Autumncloud Taylor family. Pastor Fr. Scott Herrera and associate priests Fr. Manuel Gutierrez, Fr. Gabriel Afeti, and Fr. Tony Stanonik.

Special and loving gratitude to my colleague of many decades, Professor Dr. Luz Elena Garzón, who has been of immense support over many years at Palomar College and for all her prayers for me and my family, which have been healing and faith-filled. Finally to MEChA de Palomar College for all their support during my years as their advisor it was a great honor to serve. In rememberance of sisters: Nancy, Martha, "Marty," Rose and brother Carlos. In remembrance of friends Ruth Stockton and Adrian Fernandes wonderful friends. In Loving Memory of Maria Consuelo Alcala (1951-1998). Sean O'Shea (12/74 - 12/06), MECHA president and great leader (12/74). Maria Luisa Padilla (June 06, 1922 – November 30, 2023) our dearly beloved cousin and spiritual angel of love and kindness.

IN LOVING MEMORY

Maria Luisa Padilla

June 6, 1922 - November 30, 2023

TABLE OF CONTENT

FIRST CASE STUDY

The Birth of an American Empire and the American Creed

John E. Valdez

Introduction

STATEMENT OF PURPOSE

This case study will examine the American colonial period and its historical, political, and international relations and forces that combined to generate the early formation of American political and ideological foundations and principles of the American Creed as examined by Samuel P. Huntington's thesis. The analysis will examine the British laws and political beliefs borrowed by the British colonists from Great Britain through its thinkers and traditions. I will also show how the primary objectives and policies of the colonists for trade and territorial expansion westward imbued the colonists with a world view of empire and expansion that impacted their foreign relations with Great Britain and its competitor and ally, France, while still functioning as colonies of Britain. Influenced by its vast geographical terrain and potential, it grew in abundant confidence as it sought to expand its borders but was intruded upon by the British government. Beset with the enforcement of unjust laws and codes, which the colonists considered were forced upon them unilaterally, the colonists sought actions to remedy this conflictual situation. The principles of *liberty, individualism, democracy,* and *egalitarianism* would be the cornerstones of this new emerging nation that would replace the British colonial structure and relations to fulfill the prophecy of 1760s that predicted that the colonists would seek independence from Great Britain.

Historical Roots of Colonial American Foreign Policy

FROM THE AMERICAN COLONIAL-REVOLUTIONARY PERIOD TO THE DEVELOPMENT OF THE AMERICAN CREED PERIOD

The study of early foreign policy emanating from the thirteen British colonies that would become the United States of America shows a remarkable degree of focus and consistency from the beginning of the 17th century to the end of the 19th century. This foreign policy of imperial aspiration was centered on two fundamental goals: freedom of trade with all foreign markets and the exploitation of the North American continent. The earliest colonial declaration of geopolitical-continental intent was in the Virginia Charter of 1609 where the policymakers claimed all lands to the Pacific Ocean in the general latitude in Virginia, a claim which was interpreted very liberally by the Virginians according to their own self-interest.

The colonial pursuit of these two objectives was part of a natural and sustained evolution of the young and vigorous colonial commercial structure. In time, the British Colonials shed their European identity and status on the path to becoming independent and self-serving Americans in search of territorial expansion and powerful commercial entrepreneurship.

These objectives over time became solidified and intensified by: 1) the expulsion of the French from the interior of the continent with the loss of Canada during the Seven Years War (1756-1763), 2) the purchase of the Louisiana Territory from Napoleon in 1803, and 3) the seizure of more than half of the national territory of Mexico in the Mexican-American War of 1846-1848.

The roots of colonial expansion began when the British Colonies sought a western entrance to the Pacific or to the interior of the unknown continent, which at that time was still unexplored. This policy of expansion can be considered foreign policy related because the English-speaking colonists (yet to become Americans) were denied access to the interior continent by the British, French, and Spanish foreign powers. DeVoto explains that there continued to persist a failure to understand how wide the continent was. Great misperceptions were erroneously passed from the Natives to the French.

The British colonists, motivated to exploit the interior of the Continent to the Pacific, sought to enter into treaty alliance with or to wage war against sovereign foreign states to achieve their ultimate goal of taking control over the entire continent. This was the primary objective of foreign relations of the United States until the Civil War, 1861-1865. A French statesman, Charles Gravier, Comte de Vergennes, in 1763 French ambassador to the Sublime Porte, commented on the Treaty of Paris, which caused hostilities in that year, "The consequences of the entire cession of Canada are obvious. I am persuaded England will ere long repent of having removed the only check that could keep her colonies in awe. They stand no longer in need of her protection; she will call on them to contribute towards supporting the burdens they have helped to bring on her; and they will answer by striking off all dependence" (Katz and Murrin).

The first of the colonial settlements by the British contain in their founding charters of Virginia (1609) and Massachusetts (1628-1691), and Connecticut (1662) are indications that they sought the "full extent of the land west to the ocean" (DeVoto 59). Their objective in the beginning clearly identifies their claims to the Pacific Coast even though the continent was still unknown and not fully explored. The colonial geographical impulse to increase and secure land would, in the 19th century, become actuality as an enormous continental power from sea-to-sea and become the great imperial power of the United States. The newly formed Colonies of the British Empire in the New World found themselves in a predictable, competitive, and hostile relationship with their historical European enemy, the French. French explorers, rivermen, and traders had

Charles Gravier, Comte de Vergennes. French Ambassador to the Sublime Porte
HJBY38. Copyright @ www.alamy.com

traversed the immense territories of Canada with its wild and enormous lakes and wilderness landscapes of incredible beauty and expansive forests. Then they followed the great unknown rivers to establish trade among the numerous Native American tribes.

With the principal indigenous groups, the Iroquois, Ottawas, Hurons, and Susquehanna, the French's network of the thriving beaver fur trade was the dominant source of trade and economic enterprise bringing rich returns to investors. "The New World" was a constantly expanding market and thus a powerful force in the development of capitalism and

nationalism (DeVoto 91). In another passage, DeVoto asserts that "the beaver fur trade down to 1763 was the principal objective of imperial competition and was everywhere in the continent north of Mexico. The fur currency market of European manufacturers in the New World was a constantly expanding market" (DeVoto 90).

While the French had established a highly thriving trade network of Native peoples, they were handicapped in their development. For all their mastering of the Great Valley and Canadian wilderness, they did not have a sufficient base of the French population, commerce, and agricultural infrastructure to compete against the British colonies, which had a high degree of settlement population, commerce, trade, and agriculture. The population of New France in 1680 was only 10,000 compared to the British colonial population of 200,000.

The Peace of Utrecht (1713) historically marks the beginning of British imperial expansion in North America where they could easily use their sea power supremacy in establishing greater colonial control. This growing British expansion provoked the French to respond to the British continental strategy to make greater efforts and strategies to secure the West. At this time the vast territory was not fully known or traveled by European powers, except for the Spanish, who had made some entrances from Mexico to the Midwest and Southwest in search of gold and then went through inactive periods and limited settlement.

The British victory over New France (Quebec) was the beginning of changes that would greatly alter the course of history. The French and Indian War, which began in 1756 and ended in 1763, expelled the French from Canada, and the British added another colonial territory to its long list that included India, the West Indies, the West Coast of Africa, the American colonies, and now Canada.

"English colonies had become though not yet a nation, a people of themselves, an imperial people. Whether the Americans had completed or were just completing their separateness count less than that they had entered on an imperial expansion. As both a dream and a fact, the American empire was born before the United States" (DeVoto 228). The Seven Year War (French and Indian War, 1756-1763) ended, and the Treaty of Paris ended with the French suffering the loss of Canada and confirming Canada as a British possession.

The new British possessors of Canada were now in the central position of power and had to restructure the colonial settlements, as well as contain any westward expansion of Americans, who knew the great potential of land development and speculation. This decision by British policymakers was made to accomplish several trade objectives and to ensure the protection of the Native peoples from the Americans. The Proclamation would stop the Western entrance and settlement from the east, maintain peace in the region and protect the Native peoples. It also continued the mercantilist system of providing raw resources for England from the colonies and kept intact the financial trade policy where manufactured goods would continue to be sold to the colonies.

The Proclamation of 1763 by the British was intended to establish an orderly economic and political process to protect the Indians in their own territory and to disengage effectively any colonial claims to the Western lands.

The Formation of the American Creed

Based on the historical context of the colonial period where the colonials were already operating a well-defined foreign policy of a quasi-nation that did not yet exist as a sovereign state, we now begin to examine the subject of the American Creed and its formation in the American revolutionary period. The first of the four periods which Samuel Huntington considers essential to the formation of the "American Creed" is the Revolutionary years. Huntington states, "The revolutionaries of the 1770s were the first to articulate the American Creed on a national basis, and they were generally successful in effecting major changes in American institutions" (Ikenberry 222), referring to the monumental declaration of the colonials to seek freedom from Great Britain, her British parliament and hated ministries.

According to Huntington's thesis, the American Creed reflects the unique and shining spirit of American idealism that institutionalizes the values of *liberalism, democracy, individualism,* and *egalitarianism* (See Chronology of Events on pages 34-35). Huntington describes the historical periods as follows:

"Revolutionary years from the 1760s to 1770s, the Jacksonian surge of reforms in the progressive era from the 1820s to 1830s, the progressive era from the 1890s to 1914, and the latest resurgence of moralistic reform in the 1960s and early 1970s. These reforms have much in common and almost always the proponents of reform have failed to realize their goals completely." - Huntington's article: American Ideals versus American Institutions third edition by G. John Ibenkerry's book American Foreign Policy.

Political Turmoil of the American British Colonials

While these extraordinary principles were formulated in the Revolutionary era, the great majority of British colonials in America were far from wholeheartedly accepting independence and separation from their royal heritage and the bond with their beloved mother country, Great Britain. Saville documents in his work "Nationalism and other Loyalties in the American Revolution," the anguished political and psychological duress that many British loyalists and colonists endured concerning separation from Great Britain. Whigs and colonists alike, except for the smaller number of passionate radicals like Thomas Paine, Samuel Adams, and John Hancock. The Radicals who were beginning to espouse separation from Great Britain were at the same time formulating what would become the American Creed. Although at this time the institutions reflected the reality of public sentiment, the majority's loyalty was to the Crown; thus we see the dichotomy between the evolving American Creed and the reality of public opinion was wide.[1]

An important lack of a "national policy" by the American colonies and their development was why the colonies as an entity were not recognized by the British ministry officials who were given the responsibility to oversee and manage the colonies in America. It was abundantly evident to astute French statesmen, such as Vergennes, who were scrutinizing the expanding American colonies on the path of becoming a world power (DeVoto).

The following will identify factors that reveal ineffective leadership by the British ministries, which provoked the colonials into confrontation. That confrontation would lead to revolution and the political basis and formation of the American Creed. The resulting confrontation would fulfill the conditions, which Huntington describes in the following words, "The nature of American political institutions could more closely approximate American ideals, thereby reducing the gap between them" (Huntington 221). The gap between American institutions and ideals would be bridged by rejecting the entire system of the British government and putting in its place a new national model, embodied by the Constitution of 1787.

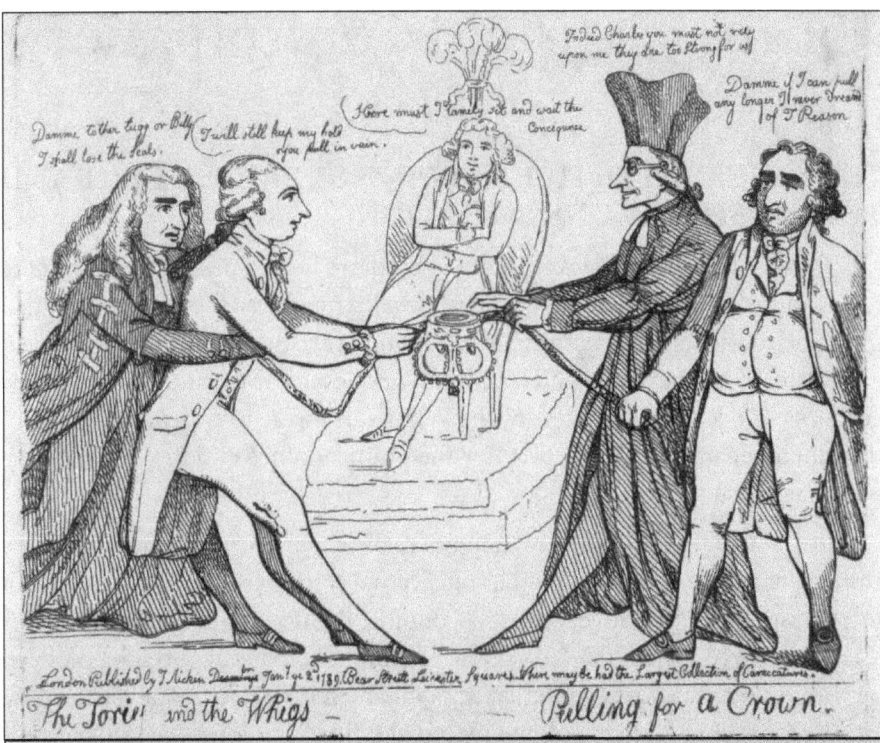

The Tories and the Whigs Pulling for a Crown. The Prince of Wales, son of George III, is depicted seated with his arms folded awaiting the resolution of the power struggle for the English crown. Published in London in 1789, the illustration shows the Tories, Edward Thurlow and William Pitt, on the left, competing against the Whig party, Edmund Burke and Charles Fox. In 1788 and 1789, King George III's mental health and physical well-being were unstable. The parties debated whether the king's son should assume the role of regent. Ultimately, the king's recovery put an end to the political struggle.
Copyright @ Library of Congress Prints & Photographs Division. Original Author: J. Aitken, publisher. Created on January 2, 1789. https://www.loc.gov/pictures/

---

[1] The Whigs and Tories represent two distinct efforts to preserve old American loyalty to the British nation. "The American Whigs stood for the maintenance of the old loyalty to the British ideals, as they understood them, but against the policies and actions of what they took to be a series of misguided ministries; the Tories clung to the old loyalty despite the policies of those same ministries, however, misguided" (Saville 904).

British Elite and Confrontation

THE NATURE OF OFFICE HOLDING OF BRITISH ELITE AND THE CAUSES OF CONFRONTATION

The first factor which greatly contributed to a lack of understanding of the American colonies and their structural development was the nature of British imperial politics and the patronage system that recruited many inexperienced candidates to fill the offices and leadership under the Crown and parliamentary authority. Once the supporters of the Whig party were in control in England, they then began to compete to enter the political office and benefit from the patronage system.

The new officeholders were then not really experienced, trained, or highly competent in foreign affairs or other intellectual accomplishments. They did not fully grasp the British government's economic relations with the colonies, nor were they perceptive of the dichotomy of economic realities of trade practiced by the colonies and the theoretical model which operated as the basis of the British economic foreign policy towards the British colonies in America. In addition to the British monarchy, the first component of the state elite relied on their ministers and counselors, who occupied the political center and held the primary power positions of government. The monarchy was also assisted by a second component of the state elite, a network of dominant semi-autonomous actors, who were positioned between the center and society. Therefore, the power of the monarchy was not absolute and varied according to the capacity that the state elite could induce the representatives of these powerful groups to carry out their royal decrees (Stanbridge).

According to Stanbridge, the first component of the state elite operated as a "despotic" power and was measured by the span of activities that the state elite could exercise without the regular and routine negotiations between the dominant actors in civil society. The second component represented the state's collective "infrastructural" power, where power was derived from the state elite's capacity to penetrate the territories and carry out their policies and decisions. He argues that while the state elite (first component) may have been autonomous, the semi-autonomous "nature of state agents of this period so inhibited the ability of the political center to coordinate state activities that the infrastructural power of these states was negligible" (Stanbridge 60). Another reason why the aristocratic governing British elite was not well-integrated into colonial society and was not able to transfer the European hierarchical power structure to the colonies was that land was cheap, plentiful, and easily attainable. This situation allowed for social and geographic mobility among the colonials. However, the powerful English gentry during the first years of settlement did attempt to make a direct transference to Virginia of the upper level of the English social hierarchy as well as the lower.

"It is a fact of some importance, however, that this governing elite did not survive a single generation" from the Colonial America article "Politics and Social Structure in Virginia" by Bernard Bailyn (Smith 90). Further, Stanbridge states that the English Crown played a relatively minor role in the colonization of America until the mid-1600s. This fact resulted in a lack of uniformity in their colonization, and the colonies developed and functioned like small independent nations. The Crown was, however, able to manage and standardize the way the provinces were ruled. As the mood became more confrontational between the monarchy and the colonies, the British State elite was not able to set up the infrastructural apparatus in the colonies which could prevent the participation of powerful dominant colonial groups in decision-making.

The British State elite, in other words, was unable to overpower the American leaders and their influence in the colonial assemblies, which were at the heart of major decision-making in the colonies. Stanbridge believes that if a British infrastructural apparatus had been in place in the colonies, British rule would have been more effective in resolving the critical issues and tensions.

The Nature of Colonial Economic Development

The second factor for consideration is the evolution of the Thirteen Colonies into a major commercial presence in international trade. The Southern colonies produced staple crops like tobacco, rice, and indigo. They were large revenue producers and did not compete with Britain, and these exports normally equaled the value of their imports from the mother country. In essence, the colonies produced raw materials and foodstuffs that Britain did not produce and then would purchase in kind from Britain an equal value of manufactured goods. While this trade policy worked well for the Southern colonies, it did not for the New England colonies (Map/Trade routes, page 27).

The economic patterns for the northern colonies were more complex and problematic. The New England colonies were commercial rivals with England, and the mushrooming shipping trade was directly competing with British ship owners. Theoretically, this imbalance and competition was not supposed to occur. Also complicating this relationship was that the New England colonies exported to England only a small fraction of the value of goods purchased from Britain and this resulted in a chronic imbalance of payment (Jensen).

In 1772, the New England colonies purchased over 800,000 Pounds Sterling in merchandise from England but sent to England no more than 126,000 Pounds Sterling in exports. The trade patterns of the New England colonies had to produce sufficient revenue to cover this enormous trade imbalance. They were unable to secure these revenues in the form of profits from trade between England and colonies as embodied in the Acts of Navigation (the earliest dating from 1660). Consequently, the colonial traders avoided payment of taxes and custom duties which were at this time two principal forms of Crown revenue. Thus colonists traded outside the theoretical model, which usually violated the Navigation Acts (Jensen).

Looking back and from the point of view of the 20th century, it is quite possible that this economic trade question and the tensions between Great Britain and the colonies could have been resolved through a more effective accommodation, if the British government had set up an economic model to analyze the source of the conflict and had created a system to understand the causes of trade and deficit imbalance operating between Great Britain and the New England colonies. By comparing the theoretical to the actual model and the resulting dichotomy, then a non-confrontational model might have been developed (Jensen).

The Theoretical Model

THE THEORETICAL MODEL USED AS BASIS FOR BRITISH LAWS DEALING WITH TRADE AND CURRENCY

A. Colonies exist to produce raw materials for the mother country from which they in turn purchase manufactured goods.

B. Colonies will not produce anything that competes with manufacturers or products of the mother country.

C. All trade between colonies and the mother country will be carried in ships of the mother country or its colonies.

D. Colonies will not trade with foreign powers or colonies except with the permission of the mother country and payment of custom duties or taxes at levels determined by the mother country.

E. The only acceptable medium for exchange would be gold or silver coinage or bills of exchange (Jensen).

The Actual Trade Model

THE ACTUAL TRADE MODEL OF THE AMEICAN COLONIES

The real operative trade model was this:

A. Because of their rapidly expanding population and land settlements in the West, the colonies were producing surpluses Britain could not absorb.

B. The colonies were producing substantial quantities of produce that competed directly with Britain.

C. New England ship owners were taking away more and more of the Empire's carrying trade from British ship owners.

D. In order to get money and bills of exchange to cover the high and growing trade deficit in favor of Britain, the New England colonies were forced to trade outside the closed system of the theoretical model and had to then evade payment of duties and excise taxes which were set at such high levels that would take the profit from their trade (Jensen) (Map/Trade routes, page 27).

These then were the trade realities that constrained the economic life of the colonies since the early 18th century. How had this uneven economic situation managed to continue without serious conflict? Simply, the theoretical model was never in reality truly enforced. The New England colonies relied heavily on trade. First in the West Indies and the Caribbean, in order to offset their trade deficit and secure profit. In time these two markets (West Indies and Caribbean) could not absorb the growing surpluses of the colonies, and the colonies were forced to open new markets in Spain, Portugal, the Mediterranean, and the "Wine Islands." [2]

---

[2] From the American Colonies Encyclopedia [The Madeira and Canary Islands off the Coast of Africa]

In time British Prime Minister George Grenville's decision to enforce the theoretical model on the colonies after many years of non-enforcement would begin the confrontational politics between Great Britain and the Colonies.

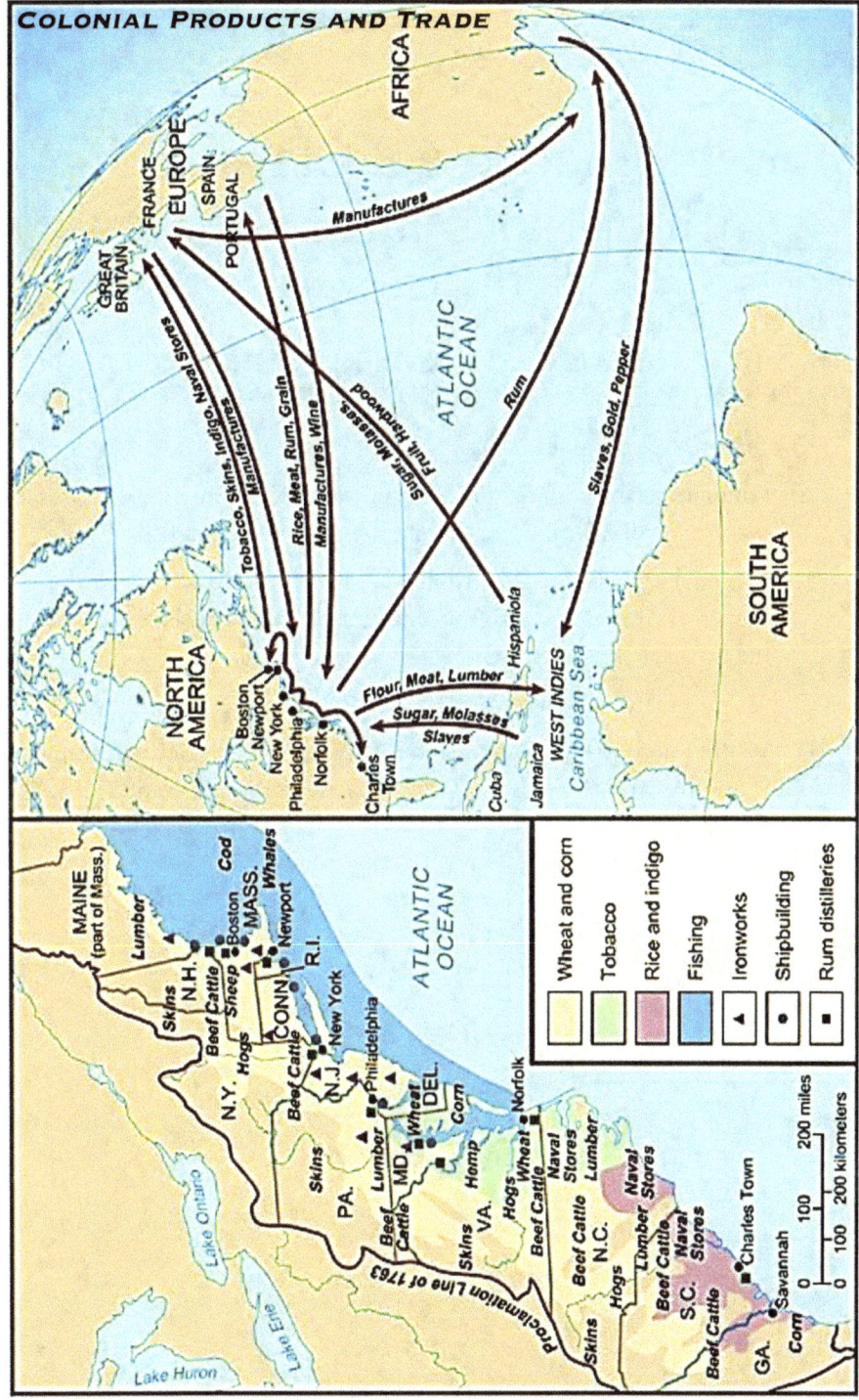

COLONIAL PRODUCTS AND TRADE

Colonial Social Class and Influential Characteristics

COLONIAL SOCIAL CLASS AND KEY CHARACTERISTICS INFLUENCING THE BACKGROUND OF THE AMERICAN CREED

Key features of colonial society:

A. Population: the colonial population was rapidly growing and was comprised of 2.5 million inhabitants - 60% were English.

B. Colonial minorities: The principal ethnic minorities were Scots, Welsh, Germans and a significant number of Black slaves (28% of the Southern population).

C. The population (half under 16) was doubling every twenty years.

D. While trade with England was a major component of the colonial economy, America was primarily a society of farmers and farm workers.

Non-Egalitarian Colonial Society

According to Lipsitz and Speak, the American colonial society was not fundamentally egalitarian since a small number of aristocratic families maintained great social and political power. The aristocratic elite through property ownership exercised power and influence over the lesser classes. Five percent of Boston families held half of the wealth and in Philadelphia, 10% of the population held 46% of the total wealth while up to 20 to 30% of the population was impoverished. At times shortages of food hit urban centers, and riots broke out. Many of the poor and discontented served as foot soldiers in the Continental Army. However, between the two extremes of great wealth and poverty there existed a sizeable, prosperous middle-class that encompassed up to 50-70% of the population.

The enormous size of the middle-class and the potential for social mobility allowed the American colonies a high degree of equality. Compared to Europe, where social class distinctions were rigid and strong, the colonies managed to develop and express a high degree of "a spirit of independent-mindedness, a defiance of authority, and desire for economic self-betterment unheard of in Europe" (Lipsitz and Speak 54-44).

The Political Environment of Colonial Society

THE POLITICAL ENVIRONMENT OF COLONIAL SOCIETY AND THEIR LIBERAL TRADITION WITH THE POWER OF THEIR SELF-RELIANCE BECAME THE CORNERSTONE OF THE AMERICAN CREED

By the 1770s, most colonial governments had been functioning for more than a hundred years. Eight of the colonies were royal colonies. Their governors were appointed by the British king (Massachusetts, New York, New Jersey, Virginia, North Carolina, South Carolina and New Hampshire). Connecticut and Rhode Island had colonial charters, which were granted to them in the 17th century allowing them to appoint their own governors.

Maryland, Pennsylvania and Delaware were called proprietary colonies, owned by prominent families (the Penns in Pennsylvania and Delaware, the Calverts in Maryland). All of the colonial governors had broad powers. They could veto any acts of the legislature and had the power to appoint all judges and militia officers. Usually, the governor also appointed members of the upper house of the colonial legislature. (Pennsylvania did not have an upper and lower house). The upper houses were generally only advisory bodies composed of the elite and conservative wealthy citizens.

The lower houses were more

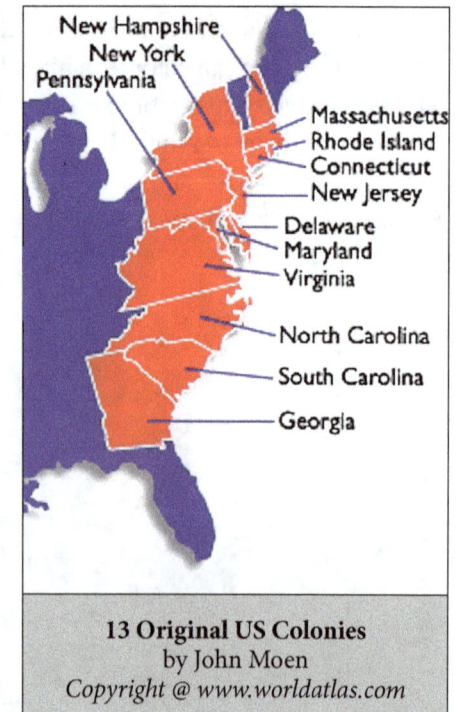

13 Original US Colonies
by John Moen
Copyright @ www.worldatlas.com

democratic and open to the standards of the time. Qualifications for office were determined by property ownership, and customarily white males were permitted to vote for legislators. It was in the lower houses where the great opposition to British taxation in the 1770s was the most vocal.

Based on the British tradition of law and constitutionalism, the colonial governments were often limited by their charters. However, the colonists were more fully involved in politics, and at this time they enjoyed greater political rights than their British counterparts. The colonists were very knowledgeable of the liberal tradition which advocated fundamental rights through law and

John Locke (1632-1704)
Copyright @ Lehigh University, Patrick J. Connolly. www.iep.utm.edu/locke

the constitution as expressed through the writings of John Locke. Respect for the citizens and their rights was recognized as a major cornerstone of the British government. The government was accountable for its actions, otherwise, if tyranny and oppression ruled, by the liberal principle, the citizens could revolt (Lipsitz and Speak).[3]

---

[3] "The Native gentry of the early eighteenth century had neither the need nor the ability to fashion a new political theory to comprehend their experience, but their successors would find in the writings of John Locke on state and society not merely a reasonable theoretical position but a statement of self-evident fact" (Bailyn 229). Foot note from text Colonial America by Stanley N. Katz and John M. Murrin quote from article "Politics and Social Structure in Virginia" by Bernard Bailyn p. 229.

The Clash Between Imperial Authority and American Defiance

The causes of conflict between the British colonies and Great Britain reflect the intensifying social, economic and political pressures that eventually became so great that they led to the rupture and war between the metropolis and its satellites after one hundred and sixty-eight years. The colonists now had the revolution that would bring the concept of democracy into reality. The breaking away from the old European monarchy system to a new democratic system was initiated by colonists, who were now in process of forming a government and institutions that would become the foundation and the principles of the American Creed: *liberty, individualism, democracy,* and *egalitarianism.*

George Washington Crossing the Delaware (1851)
A segment of the painting of General George Washington during the American
Revolution standing up in front of a crowded boat.

*Emanuel Leutze. Washington Crossing the Delaware. The Metropolitan Museum of
Art, New York. www.metmuseum.org/art/collection/search/11417*

Chronology of Events to the War of Independence

1754   Seven Years War starts when Virginia sends militia under George Washington to challenge French expansion in the Ohio Valley.

1763   Treaty of Paris creates cecessions as Spain cedes Florida to Great Britain; France cedes Louisiana to Spain and cedes Canada to Great Britain. Britain issues Royal Proclamation forbidding colonists to settle west of Appalachian Mountains.

1764   Sugar Act sparks widespread colonial protest when the British Parliament passes act that, in effect, gives Great Britain a monopoly on Anglo-American sugar market; duties are lowered two years later, ending protest.

1764   Currency Act abolishes paper money for private debts in Southern and Middle colonies.

1765   The Stamp Act generates outrage in all the colonies and is repealed in response to wide-spread colonial protest.

1766   In the Declaratory Act, Parliament asserts its "full power and authority over the colonies."

1767   The New York Assembly is suspended for refusing to provide quarters for troops as required by the 1765 Quartering Act. The Townshend Duties Act places customs duties on a number of items imported from England.

1768   The Massachusetts Assembly is dissolved for refusing to assist in the collection of taxes.

1770   The Boston Massacre occurs, and three people are killed when British troops fire into a crowd. Among them was 17-year old Samuel Gray, Crispus Attucks, and James Caldwell, a mariner.

1773   Boston Tea Party. Colonists protest the duty on tea by dumping a shipload into Boston Harbor.

1774   First Continental Congress meets in Philadelphia with representatives of all colonies except Georgia; George Washington takes command of the Continental Army. Battles of Lexington and Concord are fought prior to Washington's military involvement.

1775   Second Continental Congress assembles in Philadelphia, again without Georgia.

1776   Thomas Paine's *Common Sense* is published in Philadelphia. The Declaration of Independence asserts separation of British mainland colonies from Great Britain.

1777   Vermont declares its independence from New York and New Hampshire, and adopts constitution that prohibits slavery and allows all male adults to vote.

1778   France declares war on Britain and enters the American War for Independence. France recognizes the United States as a sovereign nation and enters into a defensive alliance with the United States to make war openly on Great Britain.

1781   George Washington and the Marquis de Lafayette defeat British troops led by General Charles Cornwallis at Yorktown, Virginia.

1783   Treaty of Versailles: Great Britain recognizes independence of United States of America; Florida is returned to Spain.

Chronology from Encyclopedia of the North American Colonies.

Democracy and Manifestations of the American Creed

The concept of democracy in Colonial America evolved gradually. At the beginning of the early colonial period, the government was not democratic. The early Puritan leaders were mainly authoritarian and found democracy undesirable as a form of government. The Middle and Southern colonies lived an aristocratic lifestyle and system dominated by their status as wealthy landowners. One characteristic that did prevail to contribute to the democratic process was the rise of locally elected popular branches of the legislature, which gained power over time.

Although qualifications for suffrage were undemocratic, the legislative assemblies did reflect a wide spectrum of colonial perspectives for a substantial number of voters who participated. Opposition to British authority in the New World by the colonials expressed the learned sentiments gained from ideals brought with them from their mother country. By the end of the 17th century, Britain itself as a nation had begun to evolve democratic institutions.

By the 18th century, Britain had grown out of feudalism and had set up a form of representative government: a parliament and an extensive system of common laws committed to the fundamental rights of its subjects. They too were influenced greatly by John Locke in his political philosophy which was popularized following the Glorious Revolution of 1688.

The influence of political thought and intellectual contribution from John Locke is very significant in western thought. John Locke was born on August 29, 1632, in Wrington, Somerset, England and died on October 28, 1704. He was a distinguished English political and educational philosopher who established the epistemological foundations of modern science. He also is recognized as the initiator of the Age of Enlightenment and Reason in England and France, and an inspirer of the American Constitution. He was a prominent thinker and also wrote a major book called *The Essay Concerning Human Understanding* in 1689. This source on Locke comes from the New Encyclopedia Britannica, Volume 7, 1986 by Encyclopedia Britannica, Inc.

The American Revolution took several important steps to promote democracy, even though democracy (in that age) was not considered the ideal form of government by many. One was to eliminate the monarchy and the titled hereditary aristocracy in America. Second, the Revolution distributed and broadened the base of social, economic and political power. The Revolution established an important model, and the American Creed established a political line "that all men are endowed by their Creator with equal, natural, inalienable rights, that government rests upon the consent of the governed" (Preamble of the U.S. Declaration of Independence). The battle cry 'No taxation without representation' embraced and nurtured the fundamental democratic concept of government by consent, central to the American theory of Democracy (Cooke 299-300). This creed evolved as the justification and apology for the two major goals of the colonies: free trade throughout the world and the unfettered domination of the North American continent. In the course of time, this creed would be expanded to equate the growing American Empire with the best interests of the entire human race throughout the world (Williams).

Once independence was achieved, the American people adopted the Constitution in 1789, which was formulated after much debate. Out of this political development came two distinct political parties. The Federalists, led by George Washington, John Adams and Alexander Hamilton, sought to implement a strong federal government with a highly stratified society system based on the independent "gentleman" farmer.

The opposition to the Federalists was led by Thomas Jefferson and his followers, who favored strong states' rights, which translated to local control and a more open social system. Jefferson's election to the presidency in 1800 was a key factor in encouraging this democratic direction for state control and helped to retard the influence of a strong central government and class system pursued by the Hamiltonian Federalists.

In Jefferson, the convergence of the American Creed with the shameless pursuit of Empire coalesced into a single seamless garment without conflict. The policy of Jefferson was to expand the nascent empire for Americans to fulfill their destiny of the American Creed of self-reliance; independence and individual liberty which would in time become "a Light unto the Nations" (from the origins of the prophet Isaiah 60:3).

The next critical phase in the development of democracy established during and following the Jacksonian period (1824 - 1848), was the right to vote and hold office without the restriction of property qualifications, so much progress had been made that by the 19th century, most white adult males were eligible to vote and hold office.

Key Developments in Building Democratic Traditions

1789   Bill of Rights.

1860   Right to vote was extended to free Blacks by state action in only six states including New Hampshire, Massachusetts, Michigan, Kansas, Minnesota, and Iowa.

1865   The 13th Amendment to the U.S. Constitution. The abolition of slavery (source from Milestone documents).

1870   The fifteenth Amendment to the Constitution forbade the denial of the right to vote because of race or color and gave Congress the power to enforce this concept by appropriate legislation.

1920   Fifteen states had extended the suffrage to women including Illinois, Wisconsin, Michigan, Kansas, New York, Ohio, Pennsylvania, Massachusetts, Texas, Iowa, Missouri, Arkansas, Montana, Nebraska, and Minnesota.

1920   The right of women to vote was nationalized with the addition of the 19th Amendment to the Constitution.

1964   Civil Rights Act of 1964.

1965   What began in the previous century related to the 1870 Fifteenth Amendment; the struggle to ensure the vote for non-whites culminated in the Voting Rights Act of 1965.

1971   Voting age was reduced to eighteen with the ratification of the twenty-sixth amendment.

The democratic tradition to have national suffrage was thus accomplished (Cooke).

Structural Problems Within the American Creed

The basic structure of the American Creed has developed throughout the 18th, 19th and 20th centuries to give fundamental democratic traditions that make America and her institutions the mark and character of democracy that is embedded in its history, culture, creative arts, government and foreign policies.

Throughout American history, the interpretation of the American Creed has evolved within the Constitution as social, cultural and political pressures responded to internal factors of the political environment. These pressures challenged the American political system to meet the civil and domestic needs of all its citizens regardless of their gender and ethnicity. In comparison to other world civilizations, the United States is very young and will continue to evolve and hopefully continue to provide attachment to its laws, constitution and institutions, which are profound. The basic freedoms grant its people a deep security that the world has never known. These basic ideals of the Creed project a resonance to the World that inspires hope and optimism even though within its core there is a disconnect that Huntington terms as "cognitive dissonance."

In his article "American Ideals versus American Institutions," Huntington provides the structural contradictions of the American Creed and the internal "cognitive dissonance" that is embedded in the gap between American ideals of liberty and democracy and the institutions which make up the real aspect of American behavior and policies, both national and international. We see the influence of American ideals as carried out in acts of liberal democracy that spread in the Third World in the 1950s and 1960s, and how they weakened in the moralism of the latter 1960s and 1970s as moralists acted to weaken the government in order to reform it.

American dissidents and critics, primarily of the U.S. Vietnam war policy and the massive military-industrial complex, attacked America's defense institutions and sought to make foreign policy and security institutions conform to the Liberal ideology" (Ikenberry 234). The dissidents of the late 1960s and 1970s were inheritors of the great dissident American philosopher, Henry David Thoreau, the transcendentalist, and the American tradition of dissent proceeded to find solutions to the "cognitive dissonance."

American anti-war protestors, supporters and student activitist groups from elite universities and U.S. colleges were involved in massive marches and protests to end the war in Vietnam in the late 1960s and early 1970s. Many young men burned their draft cards in protest and a number of conscientious objectors to the war refused to serve in the military as well. The student and energetic voices of American youth and a vast number of Americans also participated to stop the "war machine" of the United States. These activists and protestor radicals rocked the streets and cities in numerous marches to protest and stop the war in Vietnam.

Henry David Thoreau (1817-1862) American essayist, poet, and Transcendentalist.
Copyright @ National Portrait Gallery. Restoration by Benjamin D. Maxham on 18 June 1856.

The numerous youth protestors to the war in Vietnam were also joined by American youths known as the "flower children" and members of the persons known as "hippies," who marched for non-violence and for peace. These anti-war marches and movements generated interest in studying world religions such as Maharishi Mahesh Yoga and Transcendental meditation and seeking enlightenment from famous gurus of India at this time of the 1970s. These cultural and social influences were brought to life in the movies and creative arts seeking expression of these diverse social and political influences during this tumultuous period in America.

In the endeavor to find solutions for the "cognitive dissonance" or gap between the ideal and the real that shape people's lives and policies, it is vital to realize that this intellectual construct of an ideal is a conceptual tool that presents a utopian ideal, value, or standard. It is only a concept that symbolizes a significant good that represents a positive goal worth achieving in contrast to the human construct that is actual and part of the human experience. The historical fact is that the gap is the field of possibility and where we need to focus our energies. In the gap, needs and differences abound for the individual as well as for the nation, with its purposes, policies and foreign relations. Historically, conflict arises when leaders and their nations become so attached to their ideals, and only their ideals, that they perceive those with different views as their enemies. President Richard Milhous Nixon had strong ideals and was so attached to his ideals that he used all methods to realize them. He did not deviate until they collided with the laws of democracy, and then he was disgraced and removed from office. This act of removing the President from the highest position of power for illegal acts is a profound example of the power and reality to protect the spirit of the American Creed through laws and values. From the individual, state and nation, the continuum of the gap is always changing with the nature of society, our leaders and institutions. **All citizens are challenged to think, construct, question and project their views toward balancing daily living between the ideal and the real. With flexibility and the capacity for understanding, the pure standard use of these ideals might serve as guides that mark our individual ability to shape and shift toward achieving the highest levels of promise.**

If according to Huntington "the gap between ideals and institutions remains a central feature of American politics, the institutions remain a control feature of America, the question then becomes: What changes, if any may occur in the traditional pattern of responses to this gap?" (Ikenberry 229). There are three possible outcomes that Huntington defines in his essay: 1) the previous response pattern could continue on, and most likely America will experience another wave of creedal passion, 2) the cycle of response could stabilize significantly as it has in the past and come to a better understanding and be better able to live more successfully with the dilemmas of the cognitive dissonance, and 3) the unsettling forces of dissonance could produce responses that will build up to create a negative reaction that could destroy American ideals and institutions. Huntington believes that most likely the first response will occur while the second response is the most desirable and the third the most threatening.

THREAT TO U.S. DEMOCRACY IN OUR TIME IN AMERICA

Unfortunately, today because of the insurrection event on January 6, 2021, the present society of the United States finds itself in the most threatening place. The United States of America became a duped and deluded nation because of the attempted insurrection and failed coup of January 6, 2021, by former president Donald J. Trump and white domestic extremists rioters. The U.S. finds itself at great risk as its democratic institutions are being threatened from within its own nation. The only other threat to our nation was in the conflict of 1812 between the United States of America and its allies versus Great Britain and its allies in British North America with Spain providing limited support in the southeast (Hickey).

America has never been more divided and threatened by domestic political extremists white neo-Nazis and armed militias like the Oath Keepers and the Proud Boys who participated in the Insurrection of January 6, 2021. The unstable and misguided extremism and white militancy peaked after ex-president, Donald J. Trump encouraged and incited the movement. During his presidency, former president Trump and a small number of congressional Loyalists of Trump stoked the flames of racism and white militancy through his heated racist rhetoric demeaning the ethnic groups in the United States. These ethnic groups have been scapegoated and portrayed as "losers" by Trump and his followers. This is a political war waged against the faithful and loyal ethnic people of the United States by those who wish to keep hardworking individuals from living *The American Dream.*

In 2021, the unfortunate and relentless momentum to deny The Biden-Harris presidential election was a fraudulent, anti-democratic and un-American act against the political culture and institutional history. Such actions were wrong and dangerous to the democracy of the United States. Columnist Michael Smolens from The San Diego Union Tribute reported on December 24, 2021 article "The risk to U.S. democracy and the threat of civil war" after months of extensive analysis and research by the Associated Press published a groundbreaking investigation "laid out proof the amount of possible voter fraud in the 2020 presidential election was so small it would make no difference in the outcome." - The San Diego Union-Tribune, Dec. 24, 2021. Section B.

The U.S. nation faces an emergency state of crisis which calls for a rapid mobilization of moral and political courage with actions to stand up, speak out and organize a political response to defend the U.S. democratic system from future attacks from authoritarian extremists determined to take control of the U.S. Constitution and the rule of law. The life commitment from this nation must empower its people to continue on the path of expanding the principles of the American Creed: **liberty, democracy, equality, and rugged individualism.** It is the right of the people to desire the opportunity to create and seek a healthy and robust economy. Where people work to bridge the economic gap between the haves and have-nots, and the households provide a positive and sustainable foundation for families and children to give and contribute positively to the prosperity of this nation. Hopefully, a unified American conscientiousness will empower the people to seek equality, hope, and the promise to embrace the American Creed and create justice for all! As expressed in the vision statement of the Southern Poverty Law Center: "A world in which everyone can thrive and the ideals of equity, justice, and liberation are a reality for all."

All loyal Americans must seek greater adherence to democracy by embracing and holding up the ideals established in the American Creed, fostered and evolved from the American Revolution. Loyal citizens and residents must hold up the shining principles of the American Creed as a brilliant guide in the current and turbulent journey of the history of the United States.

New spiritual energies counter the negative forces and voices of insurrection, and help guide and empower the people to integrate the American Creed ideals into daily actions to transform the political and moral consciousness and repair the political equilibrium. The actions of the nation to re-balance its common sense, stability and union are consistent with the rule of law and follow the Golden Rule of respect and appreciation of our neighborhoods and communities.

As the Trumpian usurped Republican Party has remained faithful to former Ex-President Donald J. Trump, it has become more dysfunctional, corrupt, and hostile to the traditional values of democracy as demonstrated by several top Republican leaders promoting the Insurrection of January 6, 2021, from within Congress. As the committee assigned to the analysis and reporting of the January 6 Insurrection continues investigating, the report will reveal the roles of those involved in efforts to assist the promotion to overturn the 2020 presidential election where President Joe Biden was the winner.

U.S. Policy on Immigration

One possibility of a great threat could be immigration. Huntington speculates that the Latin immigration to the U.S. in the 50s, 60s, and 70s has the potential to redefine the American Creed as our nation becomes more culturally pluralistic (Ikenberry). He asserts that although this is a possibility, most likely it will not happen.

Latin American immigration does have the possibility to redefine American culture in diverse ways: socially, culturally, linguistically, etc., however, Latin immigrants pursue economic and political opportunities and seek to achieve and fulfill the principles of the American Creed. There is a strong attachment to the United States and its Constitution's democratic principles. Latin immigrants as permanent residents have historically served in the military and have achieved high military honors, as well as high attrition rates in World War II, the Korean War and the Vietnam War.

Guest worker programs have been invaluable to the United States. The governmental program called the "Bracero Program" was an important guest worker program that provided labor support during World War II and also during the Korean War. It was a temporary contract laborer program between the United States and Mexico, which was divided into three periods. "The first during World War II began in August 1942 and ended in December 1947; the second ran from February 1948 to 1951; and the third from 1951 to December 1964, largely because of labor needs during the Korean War" (Meier and Ribera 172).

U.S. Latin American Policy

U.S. foreign policy in Latin America from the late 19th century through the 20th century has been one of hegemonic rule and control which have helped to maintain the economic and political interests of the U.S. Historically, the situations or context of American policy to determine outcomes (positive and negative) have, according to Huntington, extended democracy abroad. Whereas American policy contributed to bringing about "the freest elections in Nicaragua, Haiti, and the Dominican Republic" (Ikenberry 243), in other areas the U.S. has participated in maintaining authoritarian rule, which was responsible for political repression, torture and murders in Guatemala, Chile, and El Salvador.

President Bill Clinton (U.S. President 1993 - 2001) publicly acknowledged this heinous role and made an apology concerning our support of such heinous policies.[4] Through our funding of the Institute of the Americas, we train in Benning, Georgia, elite officers from Latin America in counter-insurgency. The extension of the American Creed in the Latin American hemisphere (or our near abroad) is, fortunately, more democratic. However, this democracy is quite fragile and will need stable institutions, a strong middle class that is well-educated to provide effective leadership. Although this process of democratic empowerment will take generations, hopefully, the great inequality gap between the elite and the masses will find ways to redistribute wealth democratically and for the betterment of all their people.

Latin Americans could benefit from an American foreign policy that would expand the North American Free Trade Act to the nations in Latin America in compliance with labor and environmental standards. With an infusion of trade development, Latin American countries could generate economic development for their economic infrastructure. With American support, the educational infrastructure could be developed to expand educational and technological areas to help build and sustain a new generation of middle-class citizens. As Latin American countries become less authoritarian and more democratic,

American Creed principles will be better rooted, sustained, and advanced.

In order to insure greater economic stability and economic justice, Latin American elites and wealthy business owners must recognize the importance of widening the country's wealth to serve the masses and increase their purchasing power to advance and benefit all sectors of their society that struggle for survival.

Importantly, it is critical to any nation particularly Mexico and other Latin American Nations to eliminate the powerful drug cartels that are embedded with corrupt officials and some law enforcement members. On August 14, 2022, The Sunday Union-Tribune of The San Diego Newspaper reported on the shocking news with the title "Cartel Shuts Down Tijuana". U-T reporters Wendy Fry and Alexandra Mendoza indicated that vehicles were burned across the region and that 17 arrests were made in connection with the mayhem.

"In some cases, the burned vehicles were left to block roadways. Vehicle fires were also reported in Mexicali, Rosarito Beach, Tecate, and Ensenada. It is shocking, dangerous and a great threat to the Mexican nation and all its citizens and American tourists as well who travel to Tijuana. U.S. citizens must do more to educate and decrease the use of drugs in America and put efforts to fight drug abuse by citizens in the U.S.

---

[4] Clinton's Apology to Guatemala for the role of the U.S. in supporting repression and dictator. The Guardian on March 11, 1999 by Martin Kettle, "The Guardian - Bill Clinton has made a dramatic break with the policy of previous presidents by expressing regret for the role of the United States in backing a brutal counter terrorism campaign that caused the deaths of thousands of civilians in Guatemala's civil war." Clinton's apologies to Guatemala by John M. Broder, The New York Times, in March 11, 1999. "For the United States," Mr. Clinton said, "it is important that I state clearly that support for military forces and intelligence units which engaged in violence and widespread repression was wrong and the United States must not repeat that mistake."

**Braceros perform stoop labor and loosen the soil
with a short-handled hoe in a field in the Salinas Valley, California.**

*Leonard Nadel. Bracero History Archive, Item #2889. http://braceroarchive.org/
items/show/2889*

Maryland State Resolution

The role played by Hispanics in the Achievement of American Independence

16 MARCH, 1996

Submitted by Hector Diaz, Chairman of the Hispanics in History Cultural Organization.

WHEREAS, the Independence of the United States of America was achieved not only due to the efforts of American patriots, but also to the assistance of foreign governments, soldiers and individuals who supported them, and

WHEREAS, in spite of being an important factor in the victory, the participation of Hispanics in the War of Independence is not mentioned in the history textbooks of this nation, and

WHEREAS, thousands of Hispanics fought the British and their allies during the American Revolution in what today is the United States, winning crucial battles which eased the pressure of the Crown's forces against the armies of General George Washington, and

WHEREAS, Spanish Louisiana Governors, don Luis de Unzaga and don Bernardo de Gálvez, provided assistance to the revolutionary governments of Maryland, Pennsylvania and Virginia in the forms of arms, war material and funds to wage campaigns and protect themselves against the British, and

WHEREAS, this assistance allowed American General George Rogers Clark to wage his successful campaigns west of those colonies and also was instrumental in preventing the British from capturing Forts Pitt and Henry in Pennsylvania and Virginia respectively, which guarded the last leg of the only remaining major patriot supply route at the time, that which originated in Spanish New Orleans, traversed the Mississippi and Ohio rivers and ended overland in Philadelphia, and

WHEREAS, don Juan de Miralles, a wealthy Spanish merchant, established in Havana, Cuba, was appointed as a royal envoy of King Carlos III of Spain to the United States in 1778, and while traveling with his secretary, don Francisco Rendón, to the revolutionary capital of Philadelphia, he initiated the direct shipment of supplies from Cuba to Baltimore, Maryland; Charleston, South Carolina; and Philadelphia, aside from making significant stopovers in Williamsburg, Virginia and in North Carolina, and

WHEREAS, after Spain declared war on Britain in June, 1779, the victories of General Don Bernardo de Gálvez in the lower Mississippi and at Baton Rouge, Mobile and Pensacola dismantled British resupply of close to 10,000 Native American warriors who were a major concern for General Washington because of the raids they had been carrying out in the western areas of the colonies, and

WHEREAS, the Maryland Loyalist Regiment, a force comprised of Marylanders from the Eastern Shore, was also defeated and captured during the campaigns of General Gálvez, and

WHEREAS, the victories of General Gálvez resulted, additionally, in the capture of four other British Regiments including the Pennsylvania Loyalists, the elite British 60th Foot also known as the Royal Americans, the British 16th Foot, and the German Waldeck Regiment, and

WHEREAS, fighting under the command of General Gálvez were men from Spain, Cuba, México, Santo Domingo, Puerto Rico, Venezuela, Costa Rica as well as from the United States, France, Germany, Italy and Native American Nations such as the Choctaw, Chickasaw, and Creek, and

WHEREAS, the United States Senate has recognized that the actions of those men and their brave commander were very important for the triumph of American efforts in the Carolinas and Georgia, and also for the final vistory against Lord Charles Cornwallis in Yorktown, Virginia, and

WHEREAS, the success of the French and American armies at Yorktown would have been difficult to achieve without the donation of 500,000 pounds tournois that were collected in six hours by prominent citizens of Havana, Cuba, for the campaign, and without an additional 1,000,000 pounds that were subsequently donated by King Carlos III of Spain for the same purpose, and

WHEREAS, the Yorktown campaign consisted not only of a siege by land but also by sea, undertaken by the French fleet under Admiral de Grasse, whose ships had been readied and supplied with 100,000 pesos from the Spanish colonies of Domingo and Puerto Rico that were handed over by Spanish authorities to the French for said purpose, and

WHEREAS, an important element in the French naval victory at the Battle of the Virginia Capes, which sealed the fate of Lord Cornwallis army at Yorktown, was the numerical superiority enjoyed by Admiral de Grasse's fleet, which resulted from a Spanish naval squadron taking over the protection of the French colonies in the Caribbean to allow the Admiral the benefit of maintaining his fleet intact, and, thus, obtain the superiority in numbers deemed necessary to defeat the British, and

WHEREAS, hardly any of these Hispanic contributions to American independence are mentioned in the current history textbooks of this nation, be it

RESOLVED, that the Legislature of Maryland acknowledges the pivotal role of Spain and Spanish America in the triumph of the American Revolution, and also recognizes General Bernardo de Gálvez and his men for their significant contributions and achievements in this respect, and, be it further

RESOLVED, that the Legislature of Maryland hereby urges historians nation-wide to a deeper examination and dissemination of the role played by Hispanics in the accomplishment of American Independence as well as in the development and progress of the United States in general, and that the study of these be made an integral part of the Social Studies and History courses taught in the State of Maryland.

Conclusion

An important part of the gap in our domestic society that tested the American principle of equality, criticized by the Soviets during the Cold War, was the racial oppression and segregation of American Blacks. The Black Lives Matter movement, sparked by police shootings of Black Citizens in U.S. society nationwide, still persists nationally where police departments systematically target African Americans and Latinos disproportionally more than white Americans. The rise of white nationalism and the resurgence of Neo-Nazis and white militias, like the Proud Boys and Oath Keepers, is alarming and threatening to our nation. While in office, ex-president Donald J. Trump used his position and leadership to support these militias as he referred to the Rally by white supremacy followers called "Unite the Right" where violence erupted. He commented that "these were fine people on both sides," Neo-Nazis vs Antifa members. Former President Trump refused to condemn the white supremacists, and their violence purposely incited riots.

A brilliant, groundbreaking and major historical work that examines our nation's history of slavery and its evil system is called *The 1619 Project* (2021 first edition, The New Your Times Company) by Nikole Hannah-Jones

The 1619 Project by Nikole Hannah-Jones, writers from The New York Times, and The New York Times Magazine

A long-form journalism endeavor focused on subjects of slavery and the founding of the United States.

winner of the Pulitzer Prize and the New York Times Magazine. This important book has the potential to give American Society a greater expansive look at our understanding of the institutional system of slavery as a part of our nation's founding. The following is taken from the introductory statement of the book and dedicated to the more than thirty million descendants of American slavery. The following statement is taken from the front section of the book jacket directly.

> *A dramatic expansion of a groundbreaking work of journalism, The 1619 Project: A New Origin Story, offers a profoundly revealing vision of the American past and present. In late August 1619, a ship arrived in the British Colony of Virginia bearing a cargo of somewhere between twenty and thirty enslaved people from Africa. Their arrival led to the next 250 years. This is sometimes referred to as our country's original sin, but it is more than that: It is the source of so much that still defines the United States...This new book explores the legacy of slavery in present-day America...The essays show how the inheritance of 1619 reaches into every part of contemporary American society, from politics, music, diet, traffic, and citizenship to capitalism, religion, and our democracy itself.*

This critical work is vital to understanding the American people. It can shine a light on the U.S. nation's past and the evil system of slavery. The knowledge in this book can illuminate people's hearts and spirits to heal the nation and inspire everyone to reconcile the past. It can help create greater wisdom and love to empower society to build a nation of hope and courage in creating a life that seeks the larger well-being of all Americans.

Works Cited

Bailyn, Bernard. "Politics and Social Structure in Virginia." *Colonial America: Essays in Politics and Social Development*, edited by Stanley N. Katz and John M. Murrin, 3rd ed., Alfred A. Knopf, 1983, pp. 229

Burstein, Andrew. *Sentimental Democracy*. New York: Hill & Wang, 1999.

Cooke, Jacob Ernest, ed. *Encyclopedia of the North American Colonies*. Charles Scribner's Sons: New York, 1993.

DeVoto, Bernard. *The Course of Empire*. Boston: Hougton Mifflin, 1952.

Greenberg, Edward and Benjamin I. Page. *The Struggle for Democracy*. New York: Harper Collins, 1995.

Hickey, Donald R. *The War of 1812: A Forgotten Conflict*. University of Illinois Press, 1989.

Huntington, S.P. "American Ideals Versus American Institutions." *In American Foreign Policy,* ed., 1982

Ikenberry, G. J. *American Foreign Policy: Theoretical Essays*. New York: Addison-Wesley, 1999, pp. 221-254.

Isenberg, John. G. *American Foreign Policy. 2nd Ed*. New York: Addison-Wesley, 1999.

Jensen, Merrill. *The Founding of a Nation*. New York: Oxford University Press, 1968.

Katz, Stanley and John M. Murrin, eds. *Colonial America: Essays in Politics and Social Development. 3rd Ed*. New York: Alfred A. Knopf, 1983.

Leigh, K. "Colonial Products and Trade" [map]. *History of the United States,* 2010. Web. Image retrieved from: <http://wps.ablongman. com/wps/media/objects/1483/1518969/DIVI090.jpg>

Lipsitz, Lewis and David M. Speak. *American Democracy, 2nd ed.* New York: St. Martin's Press, 1989.

Locke, John. *The Second Treatise of Government.* New York: Macmillan, 1952.

Meier, M.S., and F. Ribera. Mexican Americans/American Mexicans. Canada: Hill and Wang, 1993.

Morris Richard B. and Jeffrey B. Morris. *Encyclopedia of American History. 7th ed.* New York Harper: Collins, 1996.

Nelson, William. "Huntington on Domestic Politics: A Review of American Politics: The Promise of Disharmony." *Philosophy and Public Affairs.* vol. 13.1, Winter 1984, pp. 89-98.

Potter, Pittman B. "The Nature of American Territorial Expansion." *American Journal of International Law,* vol. 15.2, April 1921, pp. 189-197.

Savelle, Max. "Nationalism and Other Loyalties in the American Revolution." *The American Historical Review,* vol 67.4, July 1962, pp. 901-923.

Smith, James M. ed. "Politics and Social Structure in Virginia" by Bernard Bailyn, pp. 90-115, 210. *Seventeenth-Century America: Essays in Colonial History.* Chapel Hill: The University of North Carolina Press, 1959.

Stanbridge, K.A. "England, France and their North American Colonies: An Analysis of Absolute State Power in Europe and the New World." *Journal of Historical Sociology,* vol. 10.1, March 1997, pp. 27-56.

Tannenbaum, Frank. "An American Dilemma." *Political Science Quarterly,* vol. 59. 3 (Sep 1994) 321-340.

William, Appleman. *Empire as a Way of Life.* New York: Oxford University Press, 1980.

William, Appleman. *Roots of the Modern American Empire.* New York: Random House, 1969.

Wright, Esmond. *Washington and the American Revolution.* New York: Collier, 1962.

Zontek S. "A Model and a Case Study for Analyzing Colonial Interaction." *The Social Studies, vol.* 87.4, Jul-Aug 1996, pp.177-182.

First Case Study Review

REVIEW QUESTIONS FROM THE BIRTH OF THE AMERICAN CREED AND THE AMERICAN FOREIGN POLICY

1. Identify the primary objectives and policies of the British Colonies. Also, identify two fundamental goals of their foreign policy as being a colonial power.

2. Identify the historical events that added extensive territories to the Colonies and the new nation.

3. What was the prediction and observation of French stateman, Charles Gravier, of the thirteen colonies that proved to be true?

4. Identify the three early colonial charters and their statement of intent concerning territorial expansion.

5. Identify the major industry of trade in early America that was very prosperous.

6. Identify the years of the French and Indian War and the outcome of the war.

7. What was the Proclamation of 1763? Discuss The Proclamation's desired colonial & trade policies and its significance.

8. Discuss the core American principles known as the American Creed. Where did they originate?

9. Identify the turmoil over separation between the British colonial loyalists and the American colonial radicals.

10. What serious factors contributed to the lack of understanding between the American colonies and the British Elite?

11. Discuss the differences among the Southern and Northern trade practices and how trade problems resulted between them and Great Britain.

12. Identify the Theoretical Model and how it favored Great Britain.

13. Identify the Actual Model and how unfavorable it was to the American Colonies.

14. Describe the Social Class features of the colonial society in the 18th century and their significance.

15. Explain and discuss where American society was either egalitarian or aristocratic.

16. Recall the key historical events leading to the War of Independence.

17. Was democracy embraced by early Colonial America? Explain.

18. Identify at least 10 important American ideals as you see them that will help America to move forward successfully, inclusively and compassionately into a better future.

SECOND CASE STUDY

Examination of Student Dissident Movements in China, Mexico & the United States

John E. Valdez

Introduction

Using China, the United States, and Mexico, the Second Case Study of this book examines the nature of and connection between organized student dissident movements and the changes they have been able to bring about in their respective country's domestic and foreign policies. It will examine how these movements play a central or peripheral role in effecting such changes, other variables that accounted for these changes, and how these changes attributed to the movements' efforts. The strategies used by each of these movements will be compared and contrasted, and their success in achieving their goals will be assessed.

The individual case studies will evaluate the significance of sub-national groups in international politics. These will examine the political developments that have occurred in each nation in critical periods of its history. Such developments have caused great social unrest, political dissatisfaction, and conflicts and upheaval in the government and society, causing especially strong reactions from the middle-class sectors, in particular from its elite faculty members, university students and intellectuals. The case studies will examine the nature of political dissidence expressed through political protest, demonstrations, and marches, and how the political authorities responded to such issues and controversies in China, Mexico, and the United States.

In China, the case study examines the Spring Uprising of 1989, known as Tiananmen Square, the Gate of Heavenly Peace. In Mexico, the Massacre of Tlatelolco of 1968, and how it compares and contrasts with other historical events to illustrate the similarities and strategies employed by each group. Finally, the protest movements against the Vietnam War in the United States during the 1960s and 1970s in order to understand more of what all three student protest movements may have in common and to see how they impacted domestic and international foreign policy in their countries. A final analysis will evaluate the failures and successes of their movements in achieving their goals.

Part 1: China

INTRODUCTION

First, the case study discusses the student movement in China, known as the Spring Uprising in 1989 or Tiananmen Square and examines reasons or motivations for Chinese students beginning the protest. As later shown, the protestors were protesting against corruption, and as the movement grew, the leaders began to demand democratic reform. The student protests were not simply students and intellectuals, the movement was also joined by artists, professionals, and technical workers from elite-middle sectors, and it began to reach sectors of the poor. While some leaders of the Chinese Communist Party (CCP) were sympathetic to the demonstrators, the conservative leadership under its head, Deng Xiaoping, led the hard-liners finally to eliminate the demonstrators at Tiananmen Square and remove them from the international spotlight where they were being received as heroes in the Western media. The students' goal to achieve democratic reform was thwarted and crushed—they were not successful in their mission for democratic reform, and they did not have an impact on domestic and foreign policy. They did play a crucial role by focusing the attention of their leaders in power on the new reality of modernization.

Influences, such as the openness and choices brought about in their society as the result of economic policies of modernization, were producing a new consciousness embracing democratic possibilities in Chinese society. The challenge of democratic change in China was seen as threatening to the political authorities (CCP), who had a monopoly on power and so acted to eliminate this threat. Although lacking in power, experience, and support from national groups, the student movement was a major moral force that spoke eloquently for political democracy. Their tactics of mass protests, hunger strikes, sit-ins, and passionate rallies were successful in gaining the attention of Chinese society which helped attract worldwide attention to their cause. However, these tactics failed to materialize any reform movement for democracy. Students for democratic reform and conservative hard-liners of the CCP were unable to make any compromises or to come to some basic understanding and a means to mediate their differences. They failed in their movement because there were no national associations like labor unions, churches or other professional groups involved to support the movement. Also, the lack of a developed civic society was a major reason for its weakness in helping to promote open discussion. The students themselves miscalculated their strategy of not compromising, believing erroneously that they would not seriously be punished by the political authorities.

CHINA

Under Deng Xiaoping's leadership, efforts to modernize China also gave rise to a strong student dissident movement, culminating in the democracy student protests at Tiananmen Square, which threatened Deng Xiaoping's position and power.

China is a nation-state that is in the process of developing as a world power. It became a nation-state when it achieved its independence as a Marxist Leninist Socialist system in 1949 under the leadership of Mao Zedong. China is also an authoritarian state that is ruled by the hierarchy of leaders from the Communist Party. Structurally, China as a nation-state was heavily agricultural,

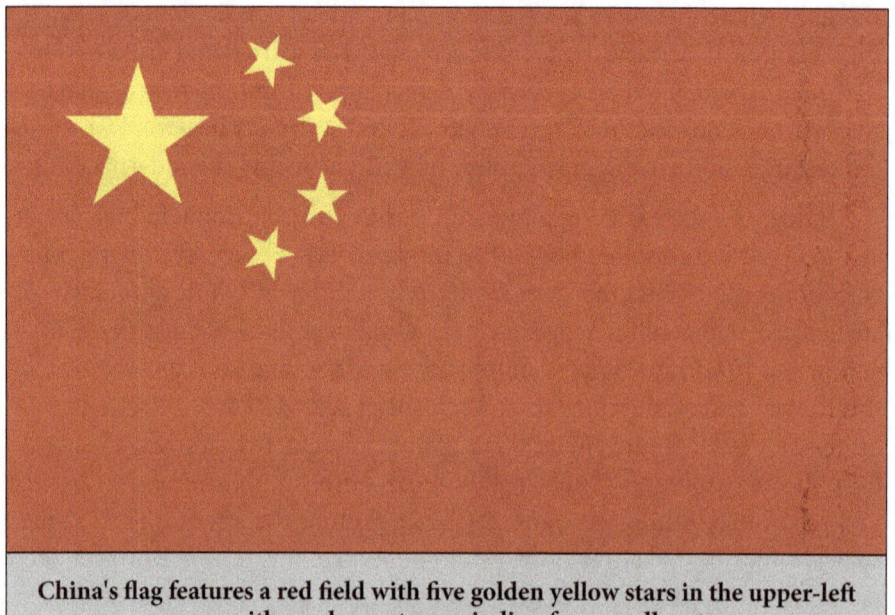

China's flag features a red field with five golden yellow stars in the upper-left corner, with one large star encircling four smaller stars.

and only in the 20th century did it begin to modernize. Even so, it has been historically a civilization steeped in its ancient traditions of Confucianism. It was isolated from the West but became dominated by western economic powers and forces that subjected China to asymmetrical trade policies that kept them weak. Under the new leadership of Mao Zedong from 1949 and later in the 1980s with Deng Xiaoping, the new immediate successor after Mao's death in 1976,* China's leaders began to address their drastic shortcomings and sought new ways to overcome their weak industrial production sectors and to develop a more even and efficient system that aspired to bring greater economic strength to their Communist state. While developing a new attitude to gain modernization, their leaders under Mao were adopting a new political consciousness of revolution that honored cultural traditions like harmony and order. Mao and other leaders after the Revolution of 1949 and up to the 1980s under Deng realized the need to become part of the modern free market economy. They began to pursue economic policies of modernization which could increase their financial potential and develop domestic markets for trade, expand their markets to the global marketplace and attract foreign capital for development and investment (Womack and Townsend). China has made great progress during the last twenty years in transforming its economy into a global market. In 2001, China gained admittance to the World Trade Organization. Since then, rapid and momentous changes have occurred and are continuing in all three countries: China, Mexico, and the United States which are the topics of discussion in this case study.

The activists and students from the uprising of 1989 at Tiananmen Square (the Gate of Heavenly Peace) were products of the new prosperity resulting from economic reforms introduced by Deng Xiaoping's leadership and policies to modernize China's ailing economic system that had crippled China's economy and production, causing widespread poverty. In 1980, the policies of Deng sought to modernize, stabilize, and diversify China's economic and social systems, and to include for the first time basic social goals, where explicitly the ideas "that economic prosperity and individual material well-being" were vital social goals for its citizens (Womack and Townsend).

---

* In 1976 due to complications from Parkinson's disease and lung and heart ailments.

The student demonstrators under the Deng doctrine of openness and economic reform, and the CCP tradition of no compromise and revolutionary struggle were following these principles in their quest to pursue democratic reform. They were dedicated to the real possibility of democracy to accompany the social and economic changes occurring in China. Their spirit of no retreat and no compromise clashed equally with the solid position of the CCP not to be challenged by unruly dissident groups (Womack and Townsend).

The student generation of China's new prospering class was the direct recipient of the benefits of economic modernization, openness and relaxed control established to create rapid modernization of the economy and production to meet the needs of its immense and growing population. The previous policies instituted by Mao Zedong, the Great Leap Forward (1958-1961) and the Proletarian Cultural Revolution (1966-1969), were devastating disasters that bred frustration, insecurity, and a lack of confidence, ultimately forcing its leaders to evaluate the painful truths of its isolationist and its anti-capitalist mentality.

DENG'S POLICIES OF MODERNIZATION OF BASIC CAPITALISM CREATE ECONOMIC IMPROVEMENT FOR ITS CITIZENS

As Deng's policies[1] of the 1980s modernization brought massive changes and successes in the urban economy and rural production, a new economic development evolved to give rise to basic capitalism, where farmers and others in economic zones had permission to profit from their enterprises and to maintain their earnings. Economic zones were created to invite foreign investment and trade. As a result, the market-driven practices and incentives of modernization created new economic incentives that began to exert new pressures and take precedence over the heavy political ideology of Marxism-Leninism-Socialism. The benefits of modernization brought to Chinese society a higher living standard never before realized. In this new-found prosperity, an unforeseen political change emerged and this new economic gain began "to erode the power and control of the party over its people" (Kornberg and Faust 38). Deng was unable to imagine that this new economic fortune would also create instability within the CCP and society as people began to exercise a newfound confidence in their new and improved living standards that could create possibilities for choices (Kornberg and Faust).

HU YAOBANG (1915–1989): A LEADING, INFLUENCIAL ADVOCATE FOR REFORM AND PROGRESSIVE CAUSES, AND A WELL-RESPECTED SUPPORTER OF THE TIANANMEN SQUARE STUDENT DISSIDENT MOVEMENT

One of the key ingredients that contributed to "the student dissident movement" was the support of one of the leading influential leaders in the Chinese Communist Party hierarchy, Hu Yaobang (1915-1989), who sided with the student dissidents (Womack and Townsend). Hu Yaobang, a talented leader and advocate for reform and a protégé of Deng, was known for his innovation and enthusiasm for reform and his progressive-minded concepts. During the first student movement protest of 1986-1989, he gained the respect of students as he sided with the student dissidents. Students boldly demonstrated in 1986 and 1988, and they never were prosecuted or punished due to the split within the Communist Party between reformers like Hu, representing the "openness" policy of modernization, and the staunch conservatives, who were nervous about the fast-paced changes that threatened the monopoly of power of the party. Particularly worrisome was a move toward western values[2] such as diversity and freedom in society and greater exposure to immoral conduct and crime. The critics of the open-door policy of modernization believed that it "brought undesirable consequences: trade imbalances, corruption, and Western cultural influences" (Womack and Townsend 458). While Deng was the chief architect of dramatic change, made necessary by modernization, he also carried the weight of leadership of the Communist Party and was wedded to the power of the conservative influence.

THE CONSERVATIVES IN THE CHINESE COMMUNIST PARTY WERE THREATENED BY THE STUDENT DISSIDENT MOVEMENT AND FELT THE STUDENT MOVEMENT AND PROTESTERS COULD BRING ABOUT POLITICAL CHANGE THAT COULD WEAKEN THEIR POWER AND POSITION

Conservatives, intimidated by modern economic developments, sensed that from economic and social changes would come about certain political changes that had the potential to weaken and possibly diminish their power and remove them from office. Student demonstrations were growing indicators that the momentum of change was rapidly moving in the direction of reform. "Many China watchers are predicting that it is merely a matter of time until the economic marketplace in China is followed by a marketplace of ideas as well as individual and political freedoms" (Kornberg and Faust 1). Deng did not think that those who benefited from the policies of modernization that he supported would challenge him, and the protestors felt they were logically following the process of reform brought on by the reform policies of modernization (Womack and Townsend). The student demonstrations were strong indicators that the momentum of change was moving in this direction. The conservatives countered the outspoken reformers, and Hu was forced to resign in 1987. However, the pursuit of "political structural reform" continued through intense discussion at the party level (Womack and Townsend 425).

Students knew of the dissent within the party and realized that they were supported in theory by some of the leadership.[3] Another important factor that affected the action to crack down on any student demonstration and protest

Map of China.
Copyright @ 1997 MAGELLAN Geographix[SM] (805)685-3100. www.maps.com

against the government was the idea that Chinese civilization was embedded, culturally and traditionally, in the concepts of order and harmony. Confucian teachings inspired cultivated persons to seek harmony but not sameness.

The leadership of the Communist Party and government had to follow the party line and maintain discipline and order. Leadership at the top of the Communist Party was led mostly by older leaders of the Mao regime period, a regime that had experienced periods of intense struggle, hardship, sacrifice and suffering. They were dedicated to the revolution and to the dictates of revolutionary struggle. Another major component of this Maoist political culture and tradition was not to compromise.

In their eighties, Deng and his fellow party members looked down upon student activists, referring to them as Wa Wa (children). Deng felt they were spoiled, brash and unreasonable, for his administration had provided generous resources for their education and had allowed them to write and read according to their conscience.[4] Seen as ungrateful activists by Deng and his group, they felt that these student activists did not know their place. Deng believed that misusing the gifts of education and special privilege, including the permission to travel about, constituted insincerity on the part of students (Salisbury). The generational gap widened as students continued with their demands for reform, focusing especially on corruption and fraud. In the latter phase of the demonstrations, students expanded their dissident activities to include the struggle for democracy.

The two major ideological components in Chinese politics were a revolutionary struggle and a non-compromising political response toward all opposition. The Communist Party structure maintained order and control in the midst of the democracy movement, whose leaders were determined, if necessary, to give their lives for reform and democracy. Further, Deng was greatly agitated at the height of his political career, when Mikhail Gorbachev, who was visiting China for the fortieth anniversary of the Communist Party, remarked, "I could not figure out who was in charge" (Salisbury 166). Gorbachev was referring to the appearance of disorganization at the height of the uprising at Tiananmen in 1989. His comment pointed to the split within the party leadership and caused embarrassment to Deng, a threat to his leadership, and a loss of face in the public and international view. Deng's anger towards the students and their democratic movement reinforced his negativity and lack of tolerance for their zealous criticism of the government, and he was aware that support for the demonstration was beginning to spread to other parts of

China (Salisbury). Deng felt even more alienated, and government plans for repression by the People's Liberation Army suddenly became even more of a reality.[5]

On April 15, 1986, the conservatives or hard-liners forced the resignation of Hu Yuobang, and their attacks on reformers continued. These developments were a serious setback for the student movement until April 15, 1989, when Hu suffered from a fatal heart attack at a Politburo meeting in China. Hu was just under 5ft tall, open to reform and fresh ideas. Strategically, the day after his death, student leaders organized a symbolic demonstration honoring Hu. The students and followers held a commemorative march to honor their greatest ally, Hu, who was their symbol of tolerance and a believer in the students' fight for reform. The demonstration gave Tiananmen Square people and students a chance to express grief, but also their frustration over the lack of political reform and the rise of corruption. This event became the driving force needed to revive their efforts and generate widespread support for their cause, which began in 1986 as a protest over government corruption and then became demands for democratic reform. Hu's death was a catalyst for reviving the democracy movement, and the political authorities were helpless to stop the demonstration that was honoring such a major party leader (Womack and Townsend).[6]

The student demonstrators under the Deng doctrine of openness and economic reform and the CCP tradition of no compromise and revolutionary struggle were mediating these principles in their quest to pursue democratic reform. They were dedicated to the real possibility of democracy to accompany the social and economic changes occurring in China. Their spirit of no retreat and no compromise clashed equally with the solid position of the CCP not to be challenged by unruly dissident groups.

Hu Yuobang's funeral was seven days after his passing on April 22, 1989. On the same day over 50,000 students converged on Tiananmen Square. The gathering lasted for about an hour, ending in violence and squashing students' hopes for greater openness in economic development.

An important factor in the student dissident movement in China was the content of membership. The dissidents numbered far more than just students; however, students were certainly a major part of the demonstrations for reform and democracy. Students were the original leaders and the principal group in 1986 who led the student demonstration. They were joined in time by other elites, such as intellectuals and artists and others from technical and professional backgrounds who were sympathetic towards the demonstrators who were demanding democratic reform. The active leadership at Tiananmen Square who directed the protest and its operation were principally student leaders. They were part of an elite intellectual core of society, and many of them came from prestigious universities.[7] Students were joined by professional intellectuals outside the Communist Party who were searching for new roles in a changing society. Soon supporters came from all walks of life, including blue-collar workers, government officials, service personnel and even some party cadres (Kornberg and Faust; Womack and Townsend).

According to Womack and Townsend, after party leader and moderate Zhao Ziyang mollified students in a speech on May 4, 1989 in Beijing, where he defended the students as patriots in response to a negative editorial published in the *People's Daily*, April 26, 1989, and the students gained more support from journalists, social scientists and even police groups, many of whom backed the demonstrators. The counter to the government attack in the media was offset by Zhao's speech in support of students, and the movement sustained its equilibrium. Students had been used to receiving verbal criticism, but formerly no severe violence or corporal punishment had been used to stop them. Also, they counted on safety and protection because of the presence of the international media, which was in Beijing for China's fortieth anniversary, and they planned to take full advantage of this important moment in China's history (Womack and Townsend).

In addition, certain sympathetic army leaders and army units were stationed around Beijing. Deng and the conservatives who were hostile to the demonstrators were monitoring the developments at Tiananmen Square and were alarmed over the increasing support for the protestors, who began to spread into the provinces. When the attack on Tiananmen came on June 4, 1989, and as word spread of the shooting of students and Beijingers, riots and demonstrations erupted at Nanchang, Changsha, Shanghai, Chengdu and Hong Kong to a smaller degree.[8]

MILITARY CRACKDOWN ON DEMONSTRATORS AT TIANANMEN SQUARE ON JUNE 04, 1989

The military orders to crack down on demonstrators in Tiananmen Square were carried out as a preemptive action to contain the threatening unrest. Students and their supporters in other provinces were aware of the demonstration in Beijing, but because of logistics and distance, gave only token sympathetic demonstrations but supported the cause of student demonstrators. When the crackdown hit, they were demoralized and unable to give any effective support to the demonstrators in Beijing. As China had no other national labor unions or national churches, no labor or church organizations were part of the democracy reform movement that could add further legitimacy to their cause. An unexpected and striking appearance and an act of great defiance was the one male individual who defiantly obstructed the people's Liberation Army's massive tank from advancing at Tiananmen Square. He was an archaeology student named Wang Weilin who bravely stood in front of the enormous tank army and stopped them at the square. The surreal photo shows a real modern-day David and Goliath battle where some have suggested 10,000 people were killed by the PLA military. It is believed, but not corroborated, that 19-year-old Wang Weilin was either executed or somehow escaped to Taiwan, but this part of the story is unknown.

The Solidarity labor movement in Poland and the Catholic Church, critical of the Communist Party in the 1980s, was crucial to the movement to bring about social and political change in Poland. These types of national associations did not exist in China. No labor union associations or church groups existed, such as in Poland like Solidarity and the Catholic Church. Further, according to the journalist, Rob Gifford, tanks alone did not break up the protests. His point is that students lacked experience in political activism. However, I disagree; evidence shows that within a three-year period, the dissidents gained enough experience to understand the basic reasons for their demands to clean up corruption and to know that democracy meant having the freedom to make their own individual choices, without the control of the state. Also, he states that "the student movement was riven with factionalism" (Gifford). According to Gifford, they lacked unity. However, they were carrying the banner of reform, and they were giving voice to millions in China, who suddenly in their hearts felt a unity with what the students and intellectuals were expressing. In this way, through the momentum of the student demonstrations, the public protest made visible the complaints of those who were victims of corruption. The protests brought to the public's attention the need for democratic reform. They understood the basic demand for reform and were sympathetic even though they were not outspoken enough to actually speak out, strike, and rally with the students. However, they bonded and identified internally with their cause.[9]

Tiananmen hit a deep psychological chord and heartstring in Chinese society, and it gained great support among the populace. Also the lack of a structured civil society greatly hindered the democracy movement from expanding and finding further alliances which were extremely critical.

Another skillful tactic used by the student dissidents was to communicate their cause to the media playing to the viewers in the West. Their creation of the "Democracy Goddess" was erected to show support from the West, and they gave this statue a central place at Tiananmen Square. Western nations rejoiced in seeing this powerful symbol of democracy, and they were moved by such an inspirational monument to freedom.

Because of western media and the power of the Internet sub-national groups[10] in the international environment, the world was immediately informed of the government's violent repression at Tiananmen Square; information was

On June 4, 1989, Wang Weilin stood in front of the people's Liberation Army's massive tank and stopped them from advancing at Tiananmen Square.
Copyright @ The Associated Press, originally photographed by Jeff Widener

not blocked, even though the government ordered its military officers not to listen to international news. Great fear permeated the entire Chinese society, and students were threatened with expulsion and disqualification from any further educational training. Nevertheless, many world media organizations in the western press like "Voice of America" and "BBC World Service" and even the official Chinese press were sympathetic according to Womack and Townsend. The western nations showed great sympathy for the young dissidents, and they condemned the repression and brutal crackdown that killed thousands of students and civilians and terrorized millions. The military action[11] had a grim impact on relations with China and caused great concern over China's future as a modernizing nation in the global context of international relations.

Deng's reluctance to seek any communication or understanding with the democracy movement leaders stemmed from several reasons. First, if Deng opened up the social and political system through greater modernization, it would further quicken the pace of change in their economic system and bring in possibilities of democratic influences. It would also further economic development in the urban cities, and if he permitted new diversity of thought and freedom, he and his party would give the movement and leaders more momentum and leverage. Eventually, other groups and areas would also demand reform in their regions and increase a disruptive process that had the potential to topple the Communist Party from power (Womack and Townsend). With the new-found leverage, their status as leaders would grow, and the Communist Party leaders would be faced with younger, competitive voices, emboldened by them, which would be difficult to silence. The new socioeconomic stratum of leaders who emerged from this privileged class stood to profit and benefit from the movement, and they were threatening to the party's

Goddess of Democracy replica at the Vancouver campus of the University of British Columbia.
Copyright @ Wikipedia.

leadership. Several leading student intellectuals and activists who became prominent leaders were Chai Ling, who spoke out loud and often, and student leaders who opposed remaining at the Square during an intense debate to stay or leave, Wang Dan and Wu'erkaixi (Gifford). They had to conform or be eliminated. They brought disorder to the system that was economically dependent on global investments and trade that was needed to maintain its economic policies of modernization, which if they were threatened could produce severe economic problems. Deng's strategy was to silence the democracy movement instead of co-opting these rebels and increasing their prestige and political status. He would eliminate their voices and remove them as any threat as they were challenging the CCP and causing dissent in other provinces. Deng did not want to reward them with any political, social or economic bonuses.

Chai Ling (2009)
Copyright @ Wikipedia

Following the Tiananmen military crackdown, there was widespread uncertainty and uneasiness in China over the heavy suppression of the democracy movement. There was little direction from the Party. Deng, however, was not willing to roll back its modernization or openness policies, and according to Chinese affairs analyst James Miles, the need for an economic impetus to continue China's economic revolution was imperative. He states "Tiananmen was a key driving force behind many of these changes" (Miles). Government domestic policy was pursued after Tiananmen in order to spur an economic revolution to bring material consumer goods to Chinese society. This action by Deng after Tiananmen occurred to placate the masses and create a favorable response to the government. Deng's strategy to withhold economic change in

Wang Dan (2009)
Copyright @ Wikipedia

Wu'erkaixi (2013)
Copyright @ Wikipedia

the urban sectors and reward the malcontents was altered after the crackdown. As he pressed on with the economic policy of modernization, he realized after several months the need to continue economic reform and economic prosperity as a means of "blunting demands for political change" (Miles).

Tiananmen radically pushed domestic policy to the point of overcoming the taboos that had existed towards the capitalist system and accepting the establishment and development of the market economy as a national goal (Miles). The global economic system and increased search for global markets have brought China's vast population as potential consumers to the West. China's post-Tiananmen government was heavily criticized and suffered sanctions for six months but China's cooperation was needed in dealing with the United Nations' efforts to contain Iraq following the invasion of Kuwait. President George Bush senior supported China's entrance to the World Trade Organization in 2001 because he believed that China could become more tolerant of human rights over time as China became part of an economic alliance of trade for everyone's mutual benefit. The United States has not prevented them from becoming members, however, is critical of the Tiananmen Square military crackdown and other human rights abuses (Tibet and persecution of Christians and Buddhists and groups like Falun Gong). Further, domestically, China's Communist Party's long-standing control over its citizens through state-owned enterprises has weakened as the economy in urban areas has allowed for more independence[12] as citizens have flocked to cities in search of better jobs—the government has lost control over their lives (Miles). Indirectly, more opening up in Chinese society has come about and has been made possible through Deng's economic reforms. State-owned enterprises were critical vehicles for retaining control over all aspects of their citizens' lives, "from their careers to their housing and the education of their children" (Miles). As this has prevented State Enterprises from controlling the lives and movements of its citizens since they are leaving the enterprises in droves (Miles). The implementation of democracy was suppressed by Deng; however, more economic growth and development has added to the emerging social economic strata and has created pressures for choice and openness. Indications of choices are evidenced in the growth of private industries and shops that sell once-scarce goods; major cities have department stores and shopping malls to satisfy customers (Miles).

Students and supporters of the democratic movement were lacking in political experience and were inflexible as they were not willing to compromise and were divided in leadership. Without full civic support in society, they were greatly isolated and were not in any meaningful positions of influence although some reformers in the CCP wanted political change. The student leaders also did not have a full and meaningful position on democratic reform, and as a result, failed to achieve their goal of democratic reform (Gifford). It was a major tactical error that the student radicals were not willing to compromise or negotiate when they could have. Following the negative attitude in the People's Daily editorial in 1989, Zhoa Ziang, a party secretary of the CCP and leading reform leader criticized the editorial and this created sympathy for the students. This position could have been an opportunity to advance their position through negotiation; however, the students became overconfident and heady with their success and failed to do so (Gifford). China's lack of a civic society and lack of independent social institutions free of CCP control also weakened any civic input. "Very few organized outlets around which people could gather" (Gifford). "The history of the student activism in China meant that even some hard-liners within the Chinese government felt that students could just be reprimanded (or punished) and sent back to their campuses. But as workers became involved, it became more dangerous" (Gifford).

The threat of the democracy movement spreading to the lower sectors was very threatening to the CCP leadership. "For workers to feel they could set up free trade unions was seen as a cancer that could spread a lot more dangerously among ordinary people, than among a few idealistic students" (Gifford). Students were not in a position to make structural changes in the political system. They lacked the experience in how to make democratic reform a reality. They were limited by their position and role as students. They were more effective as a moral force that got the attention of the nation and gave resonance to the underlying thoughts of Chinese society, who were against corruption and desired political reform to go along with the policy of economic and social openness, as Deng remained committed to social and economic reform but not to political reform demanded by the student movement (Womack and Townsend). The democracy movement whose principal leaders were students failed to achieve their goals of democratic reform. Their movement reinvigorated the policies of modernization to continue under Deng's leadership and bring economic benefit to China and also to use them as a means to ward off further challenges to the CCP.

THE IMPACT OF THE STUDENT DISSIDENT MOVEMENT KNOWN AS TIANANMEN SQUARE IN CHINA

Those of the student generation of Tiananmen Square who were killed are not forgotten today for they shaped the future economic and domestic policies of China. According to some analysts, China will encounter another Tiananmen. Tiananmen was directly responsible for Deng's economic stimulus which created material gain and hope for its citizens. However, until they can commemorate the anniversary publicly, the scars and wounds will remain. Students and supporters of the democratic movement were not in a position to bring about fundamental change, but they were the catalysts to deliver the message that reform and democracy were necessary, and this was the time to make the change from the traditional and burdened system to a more innovative system that allowed for individual choices, hope and a voice in their affairs without state interference.

The student movement known as the Spring Uprising of 1989 or Tiananmen Square did not succeed in generating political change or democratic reform. However, the democracy movement did reinforce the need to continue its domestic and international policies to continue modernization and openness, and economic development policies. The student democracy movement drew world attention to China and caused its leaders to become isolated internationally for a short period after the massacre, but then they became part of the United Nations' efforts to contain Iraq's aggression on Kuwait during the Persian Gulf crisis of the early 1990s. The student movement failed because the CCP would not tolerate political reform because such reform would bring a radical transformation in its society. The Deng Xiaoping leadership within the CCP believed their power would be decreased if political reform was enacted and their hold on power and influence could be greatly jeopardized. It also failed as there were no major national associations to support political reform because of the way the CCP controlled all organizational outlets. The generational gap widened the differences between the groups because each group came from diverse parts of Chinese history. The CCP leaders from the Mao Zedong period were veterans of harsh discipline and sacrifice and had no benefits of a prosperous society, while the student leaders from the 1980s were the beneficiaries of Deng's modernization policies, and reaped the benefits of a higher standard of living and education. Deng's personal humiliation from Gorbachev's comment on his visit to China's 40th anniversary in 1989 concerned the very leadership of China. Greatly offended publicly and internationally, he lost face and was more determined to rid himself of the student protest movement. Both parties were part of the revolutionary Communist political culture of no compromise. Unable to communicate adequately and come to an understanding, they had no possibility of attaining a resolution to the political conflict. The inability to resolve deep issues of democratic reform escalated tensions to the point that the CCP leadership acted to wipe out the student dissidents and brutally crushed the Democracy Movement generation of Tiananmen Square.*

* Author's personal account: In 2008, I took a trip to China during my sabbatical. It was a very interesting and exciting trip. I joined a tour with several women tourists from San Diego and with a larger number of Chinese Americans that were also from San Diego and San Francisco. Once on a touring expedition, to a lovely city overlooking a river, the touring group stopped for a break. Outside the bus, I spoke to the Chinese National tour guide and asked him about Tiananmen Square. He said wistfully "I had a friend there" and quickly walked away. It seemed to me that he did not want to say more and perhaps felt he was being monitored.

China Review Questions

REVIEW QUESTIONS FOR DISCUSSION AND ANALYSIS

1. Who was the leader who achieved independence in China? Identify the leader and the year.

2. Identify the two influential leaders who led China as a nation - state and a developing world power.

3. Identify the challenges that the Chinese leaders had to overcome in order to become an economic, and modern nation.

4. Identify the negative political beliefs guiding China's failed economic policies that contributed to China's weak economic performance and hindered its development towards modernization?

5. What new basic goals were pursued by Deng Xiaoping's policies which sought to modernize and diversify China's ailing economic system?

6. What was the Great Leap Forward (1958-1961)? Was it successful?

7. What was the Proletariat Cultural Revolution (1966-1969)? Was it successful?

8. What unforeseen political development occurred to baffle the political leadership in this prosperous economic period, as result of modernization policies of the 1980s?

9. Identify an influential political key supporter of "the student dissident movement" from the CCP?

10. What did the critics claim were the weaknesses of the open door" policy of modernization? What undesirable consequences were evident?

11. Identify the negative attitudes of CP leader Deng towards the student movement dissidents.

12. What was the telling observation of soviet leader Mikhail Gorbachev, who visited China on its 40th anniversary of the communist party?

13. Identify the key supporters of the student dissident movement?

14. Identify the skillful tactics that students used effectively to gain support for their movement.

15. Describe the military crackdown on the student dissidents.

16. What were some of the factors that students lacked which weakened their cause?

17. What was a lasting contribution of the student democracy dissident movement?

18. What is the legacy of the Tiananmen Square? Will the CCP leadership ever acknowledge its brutal military suppression of the students?

Part 2: Mexico

INTRODUCTION

Secondly, the case study discusses Mexico during intense demonstrations against the Mexican government in 1968. Since 1929, the dominant political party, the Partido Revolucionario Institucional (PRI), has controlled all aspects of power in the government and political system. Also, the case study shows how the movement for democracy in Mexico began merely as a complaint against the cruel treatment of students in Mexico City where students were beaten brutally when the riot police were called in to stop a brawl between rival high school students.

As the movement progressed, the political authorities of the PRI were prepared to dialogue with student leaders to resolve the situation before the movement got out of hand. The authorities were very accomplished in the art of cooptation and would find ways to eliminate the dissidents through political appeasement or rewards. When students were faced with this possibility, they made a unique request to make the dialogue between the government and the dissidents public on the national news. This request to hold a public discussion was rejected by the PRI government leaders, and the dissident movement continued. The focus of the dissident movement then came to be a movement in pursuit of democratic reform, where the citizens of Mexico would be heard and their voices would be given a national audience. This choice was a grave mistake and a major reason for their downfall. The political rules of the game were being challenged by students and intellectuals who were insulated from any other national associations since the government controlled all sources of national organizations. The students followed their moral instincts and ideals and were subject to the authoritative political system that held democracy as a weak institution, and that saw dialogue as a failure. The PRI, being the most powerful party, ruled with its power and had no need to discuss its policies with its citizens. The student movement could not stand up to the crushing attack from its own military and police. As the International Olympics were to start in October of 1968, the Mexican government planned numerous celebrations and events presenting the progress of Mexico as a developing nation. A student demonstration could potentially be embarrassing to the leadership of the President of Mexico, Gustavo Diaz Ordaz.

Student protestors were killed by military and police at Tlatelolco Plaza on October 2, 1968. The news and information were blocked out by the Mexican government, and this tragedy was largely unreported indicating the effectiveness and power of the Mexican government to thwart and silence dissent in its country. The student dissident movement had no measurable impact on domestic and foreign policy.

MEXICO

The student movement of 1968 in Mexico, also referred to as the *Tlatelolco Massacre*, is introduced by a background of its history and development. Student activists and intellectuals of the student movement generation of 1968 grew out of the prosperous economic policies of Mexico's domestic programs of production and growth. Party leadership and dominance of Mexico's Partido Revolucionario Institucional (PRI), so named by President Miguel Alemán

Mexico's flag has vertical stripes green-white-red from left to right. In the center of the white stripe, there is a depiction of an eagle perched on a cactus while devouring a serpent.

Valdéz (1902-1983) in 1946, had set Mexico's course for sound economic development necessary for diversification and political stability. The students were beneficiaries of successful growth policies that provided them with free tuition, new universities, and programs for academic, technical, medical, social and professional careers never before realized in Mexican history.

Mexico as a nation-state emerged from a colonial system that gained its independence from Spain in the 19th century and established the beginnings of the nation in the early 1820s. It later began the modernization process in the early 1900s; industrialization and production became highly developed after WWII and expanded in the 1950s and 1960s in Mexico. Once a colonized territory of the European power of Spain, Mexico was economically an agriculturally based economy that retained major components of Spain, such as religion, language, and cultural traditions.

Today, Mexico retains many of these traditional and cultural components, but it is becoming a modern power that is developing and emerging as an important nation-state, which is economically interdependent in an asymmetrical relationship with the United States. In this uneven relationship, the United States has been the primary recipient of greater trade benefits and rich resources of raw materials from Mexico. For 71 years political leaders of the dominant party the Instituto Revolucionario Partido (PRI) have exercised complete dominance of government and political institutions, establishing it as an authoritarian-democratic system of government. The leadership is headed by the chief executive, who controls and influences the legislative and judicial systems. Since the election of President Vicente Fox Quesada in 2000, these non-executive branches are beginning to assert some independence. As an authoritarian system, the PRI (Instituto Revolucionario Partido) was the head of the one-party government and has dominated since 1929 until the elections of 2000 when the opposition political party, the National Party of Action (PAN), elected its first presidential candidate, Vicente Fox. Fox served as president of Mexico from 2000 to 2006.

The historic election of Vicente Fox, the opposition leader of the PRI and leader of the PAN, brought significant reforms and changes within the political system today. However, the Mexican Senate still retains more PRI influence. Considered to be an authoritarian democracy, the government is the sole vehicle of power and wields and distributes its influence accordingly. Mexico appears to political analysts as seeming to be a "rapidly expanding category of hybrid, part-free, part-authoritarian systems that do not conform to classical typologies," with labels such as selective democracy, hard-line democracy-democradura (a Spanish contraction of "democracy" and "dictatorship") (Cornelius and Craig). The Mexican political system traditionally has maintained elections, but historically it has been fraudulent and unfair to opponents of the PRI. Their system has committed itself more to maintaining political stability and labor discipline but less to expanding democratic freedoms and protecting human rights (Cornelius and Craig).

In the early 1960s, a new, emerging middle-class sector was appearing in urban areas, bringing many young students from prosperous families. They were exposed to the radical theories of the Marxists of the day like, Franz Fanon (author of *Wretched of the Earth*), and Herbert Marcuse (author of *One Dimensional Man*), and to political heroes, such as Ernesto "Che" Guevara, Fidel Castro, Ho Chi Minh, Malcolm X, and Mao Zedong. The other undeveloped Mexico, cut off from any contact with prosperity or education, was a world of poverty and suffering. Many prosperous students felt for the plight of their own people and became socially conscious young citizens. The PRI had successfully instituted its historical revolution into meaningless rhetoric of the past. Far from expressing the progressive ideas of the period of Lazaro Cardenas of the 1930s, such as the nationalization of oil from the United States and redistribution of land areas to the peasants, the significance of the revolution had become only a token of rhetoric and remained an abstract symbolic expression. Political authoritarian domination by the PRI was its hallmark. The PRI had a reputation for being extremely resilient, flexible, and manipulative, with a keen ability to cooptation of critics and dissidents (Almond and Powell). The bureaucratic structure of the PRI operated to distribute, coordinate and control the whole country through the mechanism of power from the top down through its authoritarian-corporatist structure.

Gustavo Díaz Ordaz Bolaños (1911-1979). President of Mexico, Mexican, 1964-1970.

Copyright © National Archives, JFK Presidential Library and Museum. President Gustavo Diaz Ordaz. https://jfk.artifacts. archives.gov/people/4400/ president-gustavo-diaz-ordaz

In 1964, Gustavo Diaz Ordaz became President of Mexico and leader of the PRI. He was known as the most conservative of his party and administration, and he maintained a severe approach to life and its pleasures. He practiced strictness and severe discipline to uphold the authority of the presidency and its power. Through his administration and duties, he was known to punish severely those who dissented. During meetings, almost no one spoke out to oppose or even offer advice, for fear of offending him and then suffering heavy retribution for which he was infamous (Krauze). In this case, we see that Diaz Ordaz shared Deng's predilections in China—a similar disrespect toward students as they protested. Diaz Ordaz also expressed contempt for students and considered them to be ill-disciplined youths. As the movement intensified,[13] he could not relate to the fact that many were sons and daughters of the elite from his own administration.

The modernization of Mexico began after World War II and by 1968 the country was developing well, thanks to its domestic policy of industrialization and to the United States' considerable influence through trade investments, which helped to add to Mexico's stability and economic development. "The economy remained healthy, registering 6 percent annual increases in the gross national product" and "Federal expenditure for education reached over 26 percent of the total budget, one of the highest rates in the world" (Meyer et al. 671). Mexico also was developing a new capitalist class. While China's modernization began later, in the 1980s, the outcome of its economic development also created an elite, educated class with a growing awareness of political contradictions in their society.

1968 has become for Mexico, today, a major historical event with deep political significance because of the massacre at Tlatelolco. 1968 was to be the year of its debut to the world—for all to see its incredible success and stability in economic development. New Mexican leaders were anxious to show how Mexico was an up-and-coming developing nation that was experiencing success in its development. 150 to 200 million dollars spent on the Olympic Games would showcase Mexico's social and economic programs to the world. "The country, they insisted, would show itself as a prosperous and stable republic" (Meyer et al. 667). Now, the entire world would be able to see its grand accomplishments.

On July 22, 1968, a street brawl occurred among male high-school students over their girlfriends, which led to police brutality. This violent attack of the police resulted in uniting all the students, male and female, according to Mexico's highly influential distinguished intellectual and poet, Octavio Paz. Four days later, on July 26, 1968, the students of the National Federation of Technical Students began a protest march against the police for their brutality. On this same day, another dissident group, comprised of political leftists, called the Estudiantes Democráticos (Democratic Students, a group with Communist connections), began their march to honor the memory of Fidel Castro's first attack against the Cuban government and the start of the revolution in Cuba. These two separate groups both marching to demonstrate unexpectedly came together and joined into one march heading toward the famous landmark, the Zócalo (Krauze).

The political rhetoric of student leaders and demonstrations would unite and grow into one of its largest marches, up to 200,000 persons, at its "Silent Demonstration" where marchers wore handkerchiefs over their mouths and walked in silence. The tactic of silence and the wearing of handkerchiefs was symbolic of government treatment, silencing the voices of protest by their own government (Krauze). The student leaders of Tiananmen effectively created the image and symbol of freedom through the Goddess of Democracy to promote and announce to the world their commitment and desire for a democratic Chinese society. Mexican students effectively used the "Silent Demonstration" equally signifying the government's treatment towards those who raise their voices for democracy showing how each movement incorporated symbolic expressions to focus on their positions (Krauze).

The following poem illustrates the deep commitment of the students and others to their spirit of sacrifice and courage in spite of opposition in China. This same view could also be applied to those in Mexico who gave their lives to speak out against corruption and claim the need for democracy.

We have awakened the people.
We have seeded democracy.
We will win
Our next generation
Will continue,
It doesn't matter
If we don't succeed.
     Anonymous, Poems from Tiananmen Square (Greenberg 736)

In August, the newly formed National Strike Committee (CNH) represented all school representatives and was joined by the Coalition of Teachers. The new leaders of the CNH united behind their political position. "The List of Requests" was issued on August 4, 1968, and asked for (1) the removal of two police chiefs, (2) the dissolution of tactical repressive forces (i.e. the granaderos, a paramilitary riot force), (3) respect for the autonomy of the university, (4) repeal of laws on social dissolution, and (5) release of all political prisoners.

Octavio Paz Lozano (1914-1998). Mexican poet, writer, and diplomat.

Photograph by Rafael Doniz. Fototeca Zona Paz, March 1, 1984. https://zonaoctaviopaz.com/fototeca

According to Mexican intellectuals like Octavio Paz and others, these requests were not threatening or revolutionary. The demands were moderate, and student leaders requested a public dialogue to examine the issues at hand. Students did not want revolution but changes to correct fundamental grievances of the government's behavior towards its students and university. Through the dialogue, the students were petitioning for democratization (Paz). One of the keenest minds, Daniel Cosio Villegas, asserted agreement that Mexico deserved "to make public life truly public" (Paz, Is the Mexican Revolution Dead? 245). In their analysis of the political process, students began to question the presidency and its authority.

The nature of this request, to have accountability and open discussion, was what Chinese students wanted and received, to a degree, as some key Chinese

Daniel Cosío Villegas (1898-1976). Mexican prominent economist, essayist, historian, and diplomat.

Copyright © Círculo de Estudios de Filosofía Mexicana. Efemérides. Daniel Cosío Villegas, CEFIME. filosofiamexicana.org

officials met with students. The request was quite reasonable from the point of view of political accommodation and input from civic society. The Mexican student leaders unlike the Chinese students, however, were not as successful as the Chinese students when they were able to have some limited degree of access to government leaders. The Mexican students' request for public discussion of their demands did not materialize.

The Mexican leadership and PRI were famous for their process of co-optation of dissenters, which occurred in secret private, and confidential meetings where decisions, arrangements, and agreements were made to the advantage of the party position. If political accommodation was reached, a reward and status to win over its opponents into the political camp of the PRI were granted. Students were adamant that the dialogue be made public and that all media cover the discussion. This request was rejected by the government.

While Chinese dissident alliances were broader including other elites, workers and even government officials, the Mexican student dissidents were not joined by other organizations other than faculty associations and teacher coalitions, mainly because peasants, labor, commercial unions, and media were controlled by the government, and if they were sympathetic or joined the students and professors, then they would be fired from their jobs.

Chinese dissidents also were able to host several public discussions between dissidents and Chinese government officials. It's possible that one of the reasons the Chinese movement for democracy was more integrated, widespread, and visible than Mexico's movement was because of the advanced processes of modernization, and integration of multicentric forces that were more advanced in 1989, compared to 1968 in Mexico where its society and its mass communication and media information capability were still not as developed as in 1989.

Students in 1968 were making flyers and leaflets using university materials provided by campuses with ditto machines and typewriters—whereas China's dissident students were using computers and the Internet to communicate their grievances. The level of technology and media in 1989 was developing at a fast pace, and domestic and global communications were at a much higher level. Therefore, student dissidents in China had more access to information services that far surpassed the level of communication in the 1968 Mexican student movement and were more effective in information dissemination. As in China, the silencing of the media was also done in Mexico as the government apparatus unilaterally created a blackout on student demands. However, one news program on Mexican topics in Mexico City did devote one broadcast to the student demonstrations. The program called "Anatomías" did air the issues related to the demonstrations and to the student movement to the surprise of movement supporters. The program allowed the viewpoint of the students and the message that "the student movement has no intention of subverting the institutional order" (Krauze 701).

THE FINAL ASSAULT ON STUDENTS BY THE MEXICAN MILITARY, OCTOBER 2, 1968, AT TLATELOLCO

The final assault on students occurred on October 2, 1968, at Tlatelolco, the Plaza of the Three Cultures. The police and army attacked from 6:15 PM to 11:00 PM and left about 325 men, women, and children dead according to the British newspaper the Guardian (Paz, Posdata 38).[14] The massacre shocked the student movement protestors. Up to 2,000 supporters were arrested and tortured, and many were injured in this tragic event. The Olympic Games began and continued, and only one radio from Mexico contacted CBS about the tragedy. Mexico continued to do extremely well in its economy. Businesses proceeded as if nothing ever happened. "And yet, for a time, it seemed that nothing had happened. Neither Mexicans nor foreigners pulled their savings or investments out of Mexico. In 1968 the peso remained stable. The economy grew by nearly 10 percent with almost no inflation. It was business as usual. And the forces circling around the sun of presidential power have reached an almost total state of acquiescence and obedience" (Krauze 733). The economy grew, and economically the nation was stable.[15]

The repressive action of the government to crush the student movement could simply have been to avoid political and international embarrassment at the international Olympic event. The repressive government action did create within Mexican society, as it did in China, great fear and distrust, and like China, Mexico has not made a public report or investigation, although there are public anniversaries commemorating the events of October 2, while China does not allow any commemoration of June 4, of the tragic events of China and Tiananmen.

The legacy of Tlatelolco and the student movement brought to light a critical paralysis of the PRI and its government since its inception in 1929. The Mexican student dissident movement exposed its lack of political dialogue with its citizens in order to protect the party's self-interests as the students attacked and exposed flaws of the political system, its rigidity and authoritarianism, and lack of democracy for its citizens. Unlike the events in China, Mexican students did not have any significant impact on domestic policies that influenced government leaders. The domestic policies were unchanged politically. Diaz Ordaz and his government pressed on with their economic policies of development, universities opened up campuses and the students, and faculty returned.

Student dissidents did not alter the rules of the game as they tried to open up the political system for dialogue. Not able to reach out to the community and provinces as in China, the government covered up the entire massacre of October 2, while society in China was exposed to Tiananmen due to the growth of communications that made it impossible to silence news completely.

The Mexican leadership was sensitive to United States foreign policy to contain Communism, to the fear of Communism, and to the perceived threat of Castro and Cuba. Mexico had acted independently by voting to respect Cuba's sovereignty even though it displeased the United States. Mexico was developing and achieving a new stature, and Diaz Ordaz could not allow the students to destabilize the position and image of Mexico. The Central Intelligence Agency in Mexico was aware of the political fraud of the PRI and of the leftist influence among the radical left in the student movement and was suspicious of any subversive activity. Once secret, documents now unclassified, reveal their intelligence information about the student movement and Cuban Embassy connection during 1968. Therefore, the student movement, rather than producing an impact of substantial change on the political system, inadvertently reinforced government policies of secrecy, authoritarianism, and repression; and made relations between the United States and Mexico more complimentary. The student generation of 1968 has a more symbolic importance today in that they were the ones who confronted the government with criticism concerning its rigidity and fraud and spoke out against repression and called for democratic change. In 2000-2001, Mexico would embrace significant change as the dominant PRI received a major defeat in Mexican history.

Failing to play by the rules of the political game because of their superior moral position, students did not want to play to accommodate and then be incorporated into the PRI. They wanted a debate, discussion and political reform—democracy or democratic process as a society. Unwilling to politically compromise, like the Chinese student leaders, they refused to play the game because they wanted to change the rules of the game and Diaz Ordaz would not tolerate such brazen requests.

Students did not make a contribution to significant political change in 1968. They were effectively repressed by the government and were severely and brutally eliminated as political actors. Like China, Mexican society was not sufficiently developed to function adequately as a civic society. Its executive branch dominated all other political institutions. Educational levels were improving, and an emerging middle sector was growing, but the political culture and civic society were weak in relation to civic participation and were effectively blocked by the bureaucratic domination of the powerful and authoritarian government. The student marches were important and effective instruments to bring social and political awareness, but government troops frequently occupied their campuses, beating up, isolating, and intimidating the students.

THE MAIN STRENGTHS OF THE STUDENT MOVEMENT IN MEXICO WERE THEIR MORAL, AND INTELLECTUAL SKILLS AND CHARISMA AND BEING THE MORAL VOICE OF MEXICO'S PURE CONSCIENCE

The main strengths of the student movement were their moral and intellectual skills and charisma. They were inspired by principles and ideals like the Chinese students, who were committed to political democracy and reform, but both aims were crushed by state repression. Mexican students were morally stronger in their position for they exposed the weaknesses of the government and wanted change, but its leaders were angry at the demonstrators and were politically resistant to the new pressures of a changing society and calls for democracy in their political system.

The Mexican student movement lacked support from subnational groups. Their political use of leftist symbols like Che, Cuba, and anti-American imperialism embarrassed the Mexican government and concerned the United States, which was faced with a war in Vietnam to contain Communism and feared Communist influence and takeovers in Latin America. Leftist groups in the student movement were active and involved but represented only a fraction of the movement, and revolution was never a part of their platform for change. The platform remained the "List of requests." Organized and strategized by the student leaders from the newly formed National Strike Committee to eliminate the draconian and abusive police practices detrimental to the peace and safety of the students. These harmful and serious practices by the authorities were never resolved or addressed. Instead, their grievances were answered on October 2nd at Tlatelolco by automatic weapons of the police and the military leaving the streaming bloodstains of the best and brightest martyrs of Mexico.

[See Page 94, Scanned Copy of Presumed Students Letter About Tlatelolco]

An Appeal to the World's Athletes Regarding the Tlatelolco Massacre, Presumed 1968

This undated letter, signed by the Consejo Nacional de Huelga (National Strike Council), Section Puebla, is addressed to "Athletes of the World" and appeals for international solidarity with the Mexican people and students facing violent repression under a "dictatorial and gorilla-like regime." Although the letter does not explicitly mention the Tlatelolco Massacre or the year 1968, its language, context, and international focus—particularly the reference to athletes—strongly suggest it was written in the lead-up to the 1968 Olympics in Mexico City, shortly after the massacre of student protesters on October 2.

Written in Spanish, French, and English, the letter urges athletes to become spokespersons in their home countries, spreading awareness of the Mexican government's suppression of free speech and dissent. Its content aligns with the goals and tone of the Mexican student movement of the 1960s and reflects the efforts of students, including those in Puebla, to bring international attention to the crisis. While the precise date and circumstances of the letter remain uncertain, it is widely understood as part of the broader protest against state violence during this tumultuous period in Mexican history.

This letter (on page 94) resurfaced when a U.S. citizen discovered it tucked inside an old poetry book titled "Biblioteca de Autores Mejicanos" published in 1886 that was purchased from a local bookstore many years ago (unspecified). Recognizing its possible historical significance he saves it for many years until in 2025 he decided to pass this historical piece along. He gifted the book with the letter to a Mexican-American citizen living in San Diego, California (the letter measures 8.5 x 13 inches). While the letter is undated and unsigned, its content and context strongly suggest a connection to the student-led protests and government repression in Mexico during the fall of 1968.

ATLETAS DEL MUNDO:

LA JUVENTUD UNIVERSITARIA DE MEXICO TE ENVIA
UN SALUDO FRATERNAL DESDE UN PUEBLO ORRIMIDO.

TE EXHORTAMOS PARA QUE SEAS EL PORTAVOZ A TU
PUEBLO DE LA MASACRE Y FEROZ ASESINATO COMETIDO CONTRA EL PUE--
BLO Y ESTUDIANTADO MEXICANO EJECUTADO POR EL REGIMEN DICTATO---
RIAL Y GORILISTA EN EL PODER.

POR LA VIGENCIA DE LAS LIBERTADES DEMOCRATICAS.

CONSEJO NACIONAL DE HUELGA.   SECCION PUEBLA.

ATHLETES DU MONDE:

LES JEUNES GENS UNIVERSITAIRES DU MEXIQUE --
T'ENVOIENT UNE SALUTATION FRATERNEL DE UN PAYS OPRIMÉ.

NOUS T'EXHORTONS POUR QUE TU SOIS LE PORTEVOIX
A TON PEUPLE DU MEURTRE DE NOS AMIS, DE NOS PERES, DE NOS FRE--
RES ET TOUT CELA PARCE QUE NOUS NOUS MANIFESTONS EN CONTRE DE LA
GRANNIE ET EN CONTRE DE LES MILITAIRES (LES GORILES) QUI -----
S'OPPOSENT A LA LIBERTE DE PENSER, D'ECRIRE, C'EST A DIRE, QUELQU'UN
PERSONNE QUI DIT LA VERITE.

POUR QUE LA LIBERTE DEMOCRATIQUE SUIT EN VIGUEUR.

CONSEIL NATIONAL OU CREVE.   SECTION PUEBLA.

ATHLETES OF THE WORLD:

THE YOUTH OF MEXICO SENDS YOU A BROTHERLY GREE-
TING FROM AN APPRESSED NATION. WE EXHORT YOU TO TELL YOUR COUNTRYMEN
OF THE TERRIBLE MASSACRE COMMETTED AGAINST THE MEXICAN PEOPLE, AND   --
STUDENTS IN PARTICULAR, BY THE DICTATORIAL REGIMEN WHICH ONLY USES -
ITS POWER TO RESOLVE ITS PROBLEMS BY FORCE.

FOR THE OBSERVATION OF OUR DEMOCRATIC LIBERTIES.
NATIONAL ADVESORY COMMITTE FOR STUDENT STRIKES.SECTION FROM PUEBLA.

Mexico Review Questions

REVIEW QUESTIONS FOR DISCUSSION AND ANALYSIS

1. Identify the main complaint of students that in time triggered the intense demonstrations in 1968 in Mexico.

2. Identify the main and only dominant political party known for their complete control of political power.

3. Student dissidents made a unique request to the leaders of the dominant political party. What was that request?

4. What factors led to the failure of the dissident student movement in Mexico?

5. What horrific event occurred in Mexico City on October 2, 1968?

6. Identify the year and the individual who gave the name of the Dominant Political Party known as the Partido Revolucionario Institucional.

7. What political change occurred in Mexico in 2000 that had a significant political impact?

8. What kind of democracy has existed in Mexico during the years from the PRI years to 2000?

9. Discuss the intellectual political writings greatly influencing the middle intellectual class of Mexican students.

10. Identify the president of Mexico and leader of the PRI in 1964.

11. Describe Diaz Ordaz's attitude towards the students.

12. Discuss the success of modernization in Mexico after World War II.

13. Discuss why 1968 was to become a significant historical event in Mexican history.

14. Discuss the event which led to the march called the "Silent Demonstration" of tens of thousands of students and supporters.

15. What was "The List of Requests" desired by the newly formed National Strike Committee?

16. Mexico's influential intellectual giants Paz and Villegas characterized these "The List of Requests" as moderate. Please explain.

17. How did access to media usage utilized by students work in comparison to the Chinese student movement?

18. What is The Legacy of Tlatelolco and the contributions of the student movement in Mexico?

19. Discuss the rules that students followed hightlighting their strengths and moral principles.

Part 3: The United States

INTRODUCTION

Lastly, the case study discusses the United States and shows how the student movement in the United States, in terms of achieving its goals, was the only successful student movement of the three. The United States' historical traditions and background make it the most democratic nation in the world. As a nation, it has a significant upper and middle class and a tradition of dissent, in which the First Amendment of the Bill of Rights grants its citizens freedom of speech and freedom of assembly. The primary goal of the student movement was to end military action and involvement in Vietnam and Southeast Asia. Beginning in 1965, the student movement endured many attempts to derail and discredit its leaders, and their peace and anti-war activities. In addition to its liberal ideology, another factor that helped students to organize effectively was that the student movement was supported by national associations, some congressional leaders in government, Pentagon officials, and members of the presidential cabinet. Based on historical political beliefs in the American Creed, First Amendment rights and support from some congressional leaders, the student movement was successful in building political awareness and education about the military policies of the war in Vietnam. The student movement leaders helped focus attention on U.S. political and military policies expanding the war, and through the movement, its followers questioned these decisions and military actions in national demonstrations. The major anti-war demonstrations began in 1965. The Vietnam War ended in 1975. The student movement played a significant role as a catalyst in activating opinions and beliefs about the U.S. role in Vietnam and questioned policies that placed American soldiers in a dangerous, limited war that was primarily a civil war.

This time was a dramatic and controversial period in United States history, and students were major actors at the forefront of the anti-war movement. They were part of a movement that was supported by many other social and political groups in American society. The student movement with other

American citizens curtailed domestic institutions like the Federal Bureau of Investigation (FBI) and the Central Intelligence Agency (CIA) through its demonization of these agencies and influenced American foreign policy to withdraw from Southeast Asia. Thus the student movement in the United States had a major impact on curbing domestic policies and foreign policy in the United States. Finally, the case study discusses the specific strategies that each country exercised and assesses if they were effective in their movements, by comparing and contrasting the three countries.

The United States in the realm of international relations as a nation-state is the most modern and advanced, industrially and technologically, of all the other nations discussed in this case study. The United States is a strong significant power in the world and has tremendous might in its production, and technological and scientific capabilities, which grew during and after World War II. Also, the United States has a highly effective political system and political culture that was instituted in the 18th century with civil institutions and a government formed from liberal and democratic principles dedicated to the American Creed concepts based on liberty, individualism, equality and democracy (Huntington). Democracy in America is a powerful and great contribution to political freedom and democratic principles for the U.S. nation and a powerful symbol for humankind around the world.

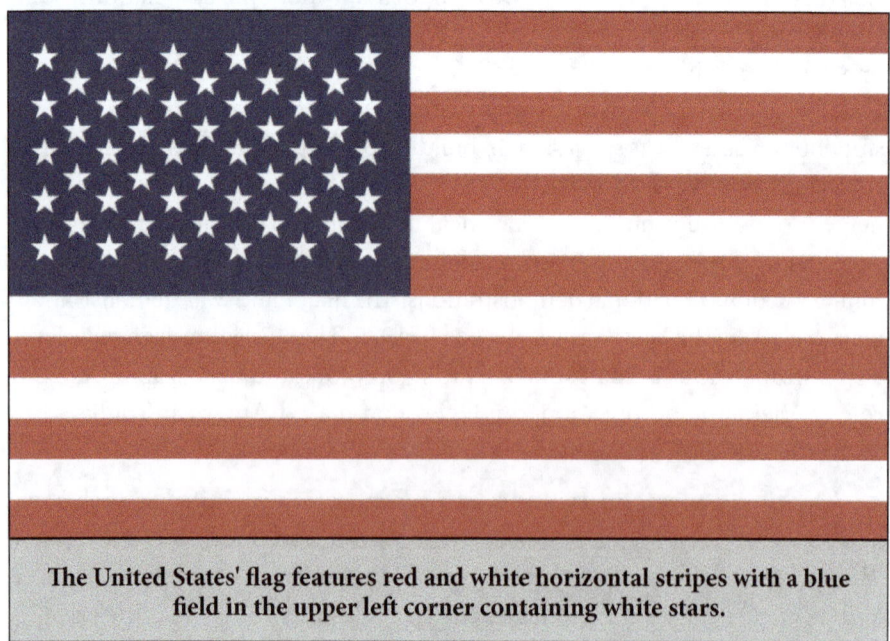

The United States' flag features red and white horizontal stripes with a blue field in the upper left corner containing white stars.

THE UNITED STATES DISSIDENT STUDENT MOVEMENT: THE ANTI-WAR MOVEMENT

From the mid-1960s to the mid-1970s, the student dissident, the anti-war movement, acting as a pressure group within the United States, was extremely active. The mass involvement of many students on U.S. campuses and universities benefited from the high degree of media coverage of the Vietnam War, which reported daily, the horror and images of war. The students were, in many cases, the same age as the soldiers. Many youths volunteered to serve in the armed services, while others found ways to circumvent the draft. Many student activists and student unions protested because they were being drafted into a war of which they had very little knowledge. A common chant was "HELL NO, WE WON'T GO" among student protestors. This slogan expressed the defiance of many of the anti-war protestors.[16]

Mario Savio, a brilliant philosophy major and key leader of the Free Speech Movement at the University of California, Berkeley[17] gave an electrifying and passionate speech on the steps of Sproul Hall to denounce the U.S. war machine on December 2, 1964. He spoke truth to power at this historical movement to the youth of America about being "a cog in the military machinery of The Industrial Complex." His passionate speech, one of the most powerful and charismatic of our time, resonated with many of the youth and called for them to resist the war efforts throughout the nation.

The United States' liberal constitution and the government allowed for healthy participation rates in government and civic society.[18] Its government maintained significant checks and balances between the executive, legislative, and judicial branches, and its structure provided a higher level of tolerance for criticism and dissent compared to student movements in China and Mexico. "The

Mario Savio, Student Activist (1942–1996). Savio at Municipal Court (1965), SF News-Call Bulletin Newspaper.

Copyright © Berkeley Historical Plaque Project. Photo credit: Berkeley Architectural Heritage Assn. and Berkeley Historical Society.

United States is, in reality, the first, most liberal and democratic country in the world with far better-institutionalized protections for the rights of its citizens than any other society" (Huntington 240; Valdez 15).

Historically, World War II propelled the United States into becoming a major superpower with its rival the Republic of United Soviet States (USSR). The bipolar structure of power between the United States and the Soviet Union, as well as the fear of the spread of Communism, had caused the USA to set up a defensive plan to protect itself from attack.[19] This defensive military plan is an indication of how serious military and political policymakers felt that a Communist threat existed. Southeast Asia was one of the central regions in this defensive arc that included not only Southeast Asia, but also Latin America, Africa, and Western Europe. Vietnam came slowly to the consciousness of the American public as critics, liberal political leaders, and student protestors at major universities began to question and search for legitimate reasons for an American military build-up and increasing military operations in the mid and latter 1960s.

The student movement, along with major subnational and diverse groups in society, marched, protesting the Vietnam War, and it helped to change domestic and foreign policy. This input from the diverse and united social and political forces brought changes in the Voting Rights Act of 1971 by altering the voting age from 21 to 18. Sentiment to reduce the voting age from 21 to 18 came from public views that said military servicemen and women who were in Vietnam facing military action and subject to great harm for their country but were not even able to legally vote in the country that they were sacrificing their lives for. The average age of the servicemen and women was 19.

In the latter 1960s, the Selective Service Board changed the draft system to a lottery system because the previously used draft was forcing a large number of ethnic minorities, drawn from the lower social economic classes to serve as infantrymen. This discriminatory process resulted in a high number of casualties and deaths among African American and Mexican American troops. This large list of fatalities was excessive and disproportionate to these ethnic minorities' numbers in the United States. "According to Ralph Guzman, between 1961 and February 1967, although the Chicano population officially numbered 10 to 12 percent of the population of the Southwest, Chicanos comprised 19.4 percent of those from that area who were killed in Vietnam" (Acuna 377).[20] The student movement protests and anti-war demonstrations gained a great deal of publicity, and this attention contributed to the debate about why America was involved and whether to increase the intensification of the war.

Beginning with the policies of President John Fitzgerald Kennedy in the early 1960s, military aid was directed to the South Vietnam government. The Gulf of Tonkin Resolution in 1964, initiated by President Lyndon Baines Johnson, widened war involvement, and the policies of President Richard Milhous Nixon expanded the United States' war activity even more. Reaction to the intensification of military involvement and military casualties caused by the war prompted rallies, protests, and demonstrations, which began on college campuses, then spread to major urban centers, and they were highly successful.

The congressional debate called into question the growing attrition rates and increasing casualty rates that were reported daily in the national news. The student anti-war protestors angered the congressional leaders supporting U.S. policy in Vietnam. Congressional leaders against the war were reinforced by student protestors although they did not agree with their methods of protest (Schultz and Schultz).[21]

As a result of the acceleration of war activities in Vietnam, congressional debate intensified, and during these turbulent years, the voices of students in dissent caused many other sectors of American society to examine and question the government's Pro-War Policy in Vietnam. Dissent between the advocates of the war and those who sought an end to the conflict appeared in the House of Representatives and the Senate of the United States Congress.

When Pentagon specialist, Daniel Ellsberg, secretly handed over to the *New York Times* secret, highly confidential documents from the Pentagon, a major blow was dealt to the Pro-War Policy. The secret documents revealed the military weaknesses of the United States foreign policy in Vietnam. Ellsberg recalls, "And being in Vietnam was enough to teach me, as it did nearly everyone who went there that we had been massively lied to" (Schultz and Schultz 330). "What the Pentagon papers revealed was that the President himself was directing this deception to the public when in fact, he was getting quite adequate information

---

* Author's personal account: In early 1962, I received my pre-induction paper for the military draft. I was ordered to report for my physical military induction when I was in my first year at St. Francis College Minor Seminary in El Cajon, California. I showed the letter to our rector of St. Francis College Father John R. Quinn. One day, he and I traveled to the Selective Service office in San Diego and my induction order was cancelled. I was reclassified as a divinity student.

about the realities in Vietnam" (Schultz and Schultz 331). This statement is typically attributed to Daniel Ellsberg, who leaked the Pentagon Papers in 1971. More of the United States population became skeptical of continued violence and were receptive to considering alternative actions to end the war in Vietnam. They sought to end military policies and desired to pursue the winding down of the role of the United States military in Vietnam. Samuel Huntington addressed the activism and passion of students and liberals critical of United States policies and those in positions of leadership of the 1960s and 1970s. These core values, which propelled the passion of students and liberals, were fundamentally rooted in historic traditions of "English and American revolutionary experiences in seventeenth-century Protestant moralism and eighteenth-century liberal rationalism" (Huntington 227).

The extent of the anti-war movement was very powerful and widely manifest in the United States because of its unique historical development. The openness of criticism and protest over Vietnam stems from the basic and fundamental ideology of the American Creed defined as **equality, liberty, individualism, and democracy**. At its inception, Huntington states, "It was assumed that the foreign-policy institutions would reflect the basic values of the pre-existing and overwhelming preponderant ideology" (Huntington 233). According to Huntington, "Yet precisely these institutions – foreign and intelligence services military and police forces- have functional imperatives that conflict most sharply and dramatically with the liberal-democratic values of the American Creed (Huntington 233). The political division within the United States over the Vietnam War between many of its citizens and the government and its institutions is a classic example of what Huntington refers to in his reference to functional imperatives conflicting with liberal-democratic values. The ideological conflict over Vietnam aroused a passionate protest and pressure that challenged the U.S. leadership of the government to end the war during the 1960s and 1970s and "to make the foreign policy and security institution conform to the requirements of the liberal ideology" (Huntington 234).

The movement to end the Vietnam War was powerful and involved all segments of American society, not simply students and intellectuals. In contrast, Chinese and Mexican movements were comprised of young, inexperienced students, coming primarily from the middle class. These young, educated dissidents were kept in isolation by their governments. The United States' liberal traditions and institutions, plus the coverage of the media, allowed open dissent, criticism, and protest from radical students. Many of these young activists belonged to groups such as Students For a Democratic Society. Other diverse political activist groups were made up of parents, veteran military from Vietnam, religious and women's coalitions, and ethnic minorities, primarily African and Mexican American. Also, some United States politicians, leaders, artists, and peace groups converged to make protests. Even further, alternative or underground newspapers appeared on many campuses and in various communities. These publications wrote anti-US views and criticized the war.

Anti-war marches occurred in all major American cities. Marches were used as a major weapon to gain attention and publicity, in the same way, that they had been utilized in Mexico and in China, but on a smaller scale. Americans from all socio-economic levels and classes joined to question the war and its eventual negative impact on "The Central Intelligence Agency (CIA), Federal Bureau of Investigation (FBI)." [22] The United States government specifically attempted to discredit and harass the anti-war leaders and "the new left youth group involved in anti-Vietnam activity" (Schultz and Schultz 303). The government fought the activists' stance against defense spending, the use of military force abroad, the military-industrial complex, and the imperial presidency attempting to expose weaken, and dismantle, or abolish the institutions that protected their liberal society against foreign threats" (Huntington 234).

The student movement with its many intellectuals brought attention to the split in American politics between the left and the right. Radical psychodramatic tactics of guerrilla theater groups, acting out and dramatizing violence and destruction, conveyed visual and emotional responses from society, causing it to question the morality of war against unknown people. Nathan Glazer believed that these and other radical tactics did reach segments of the population and "played a major role in changing American policy in Vietnam" (Glazer 3).

Intimidation by radical students and militancy of African American groups created tensions toward supporters of government policies, as reported in the national media during the later 1960s. Berkeley radicals sat down in front of trains to prevent them from bringing recruits to the Oakland Induction Station. Also, radical students from San Diego created log piles on the tracks near Del Mar, California to stop the transportation of tanks to the San Diego area, according to local news media. In the early 1970s, student movement leaders and intellectuals developed enormous power and were connected to all segments of American society and impacted lifestyles, politics, and domestic and internal policies (Schultz and Schultz).

Student activists were a central part of the anti-war movement and had radicalized US campuses and universities, creating the setting for the tragedy of Kent State.[23] In the United States, the most modern and advanced country, with all its dominant institutions of power – the university, society, and state, converged to question and end United States war policy in Vietnam. This action established the university as a major focus in American politics.

"Another important aspect of student movements is that they feel a kinship with the exploited people in society. Feuer points out also that students in traditional societies are attempting to dethrone the elder generation and symbolically their fathers" (Feuer 19). According to Feuer, the student activists, empathically identify with the oppressed peoples under attack. Feuer's belief is that the student activists are acting out at a deeper psychological level and that

Bread and puppet theater: Greenwich Village (New York, N.Y.): Anti-war protest (1965)
Copyright © Robert Joyce papers, 1952-1973, Historical Collections and Labor Archives, Special Collections Library, University Libraries, Pennsylvania State University.

Masked Members of The Bread and Puppet Theater stage a protest of the Vietnam War in Washington Square.
Copyright © Fred W. McDarrah.
March 15, 1965.

their defiance against authority and those in power stems from their anguish and desire to strike out against their elders in positions of power.

The United States student movement had the highest number of developing alliances and connections with subnational groups from religious groups, some unions, political leaders, critics of the government, and the mainstream of the American middle class. The American student movement maintained a diverse level of support from all sectors of society, and all nations being examined in this paper had the most profound impact on domestic and foreign policy. The United States as the most advanced and modernized political system was able to permit the anti-war movement to have its own voice of dissent. Thus at significant levels, the student movement and all other dissenting alliances changed internal domestic policy and external foreign policy. This movement had one significant element called the "new moralism" articulated by Huntington that ignited the creedal passion of Americans and released the voice of dissent never before experienced in America.

"The Vietnam War evoked a clash unprecedented in American affairs," Tom Wells writes, noting that "never before had so many U.S. citizens defied their leaders during wartime. National protests began in April 1965 with an anti-war rally sponsored by Students For A Democratic Society. As the war intensified, outrage grew, sparking demonstrations, sit-ins, teach-ins, student strikes, draft-card burnings, electoral campaigns, fasts, lobbying, vigils, and dramatic street theater. Throughout the Spring Mobilization, the New Mobilization, the Student Mobilization, and more, activists alternated between exhilaration and each larger, more insistent demonstration and anger and exasperation at the escalation of the war that often followed. Nevertheless, Wells contends the movement "played a major role in constraining, de-escalating and ending the war" (Schultz and Schultz 274).

The mass protest and growing anti-war movement in the United States waged by its mobilized citizens became an important factor that greatly influenced the Vietnam War policy and was a major force in curbing the institutional leadership and forces of government. "In the United States sentiment against the undeclared war mounted steadily. Peace marches, demonstrations, and rallies protesting American involvement in what was essentially a civil war were organized across the land. Intellectuals, church figures, businessmen, youth, and the elderly took part in vigils and acts of civil disobedience to show their disapproval of the war. In Congress and even in the Pentagon and the

Presidential Cabinet some began to question the legitimacy and wisdom of U.S. actions in Southeast Asia" (Encyclopedia Britannica 362).

The anti-war movement protestors through their passion to end the war were exercising the freedoms of the First Amendment mainly freedom of speech and freedom of assembly and because they were so effective in their protests and deeply felt moralism against the war, they created to some extent an impotent government. "Yet the continual presence of deeply felt moralistic sentiments among major groups in American society could continue to ensure weak and divided government, devoid of authority and unable to deal satisfactorily with the economic, social, and foreign challenges confronting the nation" (Huntington 230).

The student movement with the other major associations from the local, state, and national levels combined in a united movement never before seen, and effectively through their strategies of protest marches, rallies, and civil disobedience forced the government and its leaders to de-escalate the war in Vietnam and also constrained the government's institutions like the FBI and CIA. Therefore, the United States student movement was the only successful student movement of the three case studies. The success of the student movement functioning as a dissident movement in society was because of its liberal heritage and more highly developed civic society and independent political institutions. Its higher and advanced levels of democracy allowed the citizens and student activists to exercise their amendment rights to pressure their government peacefully to end the war in Vietnam.

Rosati and Twing, writing on the decline of presidential power since Vietnam at the end of the Cold War, mention that the Vietnam tragedy and Watergate symbolized the end of the extraordinary power that presidents enjoyed in making foreign policy. Further, they add that the dominant anti-Communist consensus that existed throughout the government and society no longer could survive the impact and reality of the Vietnam War. Its collapse produced a reasserting Congress, new and varied interest groups and social movements, a more critical press, and an American cynical public. Rosati and Twing assert that presidential power has regressed substantially since Vietnam at the end of the Cold War. The post-Vietnam years also symbolized and accelerated the weakening of America's power over other world actors in the international political economy.

CHINA AND MEXICO ON COLLISION COURSE AGAINST THE PURE CONSCIENCE OF SOCIETY

In contrast, the economic forces of modernization and economic policies were central to the survival and development of China and Mexico as modern nation-states. Economic gaps still persisted between the new aspiring middle sector and the poor. The movement toward modernization in these countries opened up new incentives for profit, new choices for material goods, and a newly found confidence and greed among the prosperous new elites, as well as a willingness to question the inequities in their societies, both traditional and modern. In time the youth of the middle sector, possessing the advantages of university education, were able to formulate critical questions about the political process. Their stinging criticism elevated over time the threats of repression from their governments. The authoritarian structures of China and Mexico did not allow for genuine dialogue between their governments and their country's citizens. A high degree of government intolerance towards its citizens and students did not allow for dissent in their political systems. Civic participation and involvement, not sanctioned by the governments, were weak. Only associations and unions controlled by the government were recognized. Also, technology was not as advanced as it would be in the 1980s. The progress of the information age was just tuning up, so the movement in Mexico could still be controlled and isolated. The movement in China was impossible to keep silenced since the technology of the computer and the Internet announced to the world the tragedy and events of the uprising. The role of the media to influence truth would also be challenged by the opposite force to misinform and corrupt the truth.

Both China and Mexico's political authorities were focused on maintaining their monopolies of power; they did not tolerate any dissent, especially dissent from any of its inexperienced, fearless, and idealistic students. The power of the elites collided with the power of the youth, who had only their idealistic principles of democracy. Feuer in his analysis of student movements maintains that "in the first place, a student movement, unlike a labor movement, has at its inception only a vague sense of its immediate goals; indeed its ultimate aims" are usually inchoate (Feuer 19; Valdez, Modern Latin American History Research Paper)[24]. Feuer also points out that a student movement comes out of the "diffused feeling of opposition to things as they are" (Feuer 20). Again he relates that student movements adopt the attitude that they are "The only ones who can do it" in their quest for social justice. Also, students feel that because of the temporary stations in life as students that they reflect "The pure conscience of society" (Feuer 20).

Economically, the United States, in comparison to China, was enormous. The United States at the beginning of the 1990s had the world's largest economy. In 1987 its gross national product (GNP), or the total value of all goods and services produced was calculated at 4,527 billion" (Ranney 567). During the Cold War period and the Vietnam War, the national priority was to maintain a strategic defense against its enemies through the development of sophisticated weapons systems, such as anti-ballistic missiles (ABM) and the multiple independently targeted re-entry vehicle (MIRV). These weapons were costly systems that were known according to expert testimony not to work, but were approved to maintain the production for profit. The driving force behind these decisions of weapons procurement was "to maintain jobs, profits for businessmen and power for bureaucrats." Such policies on weapons defense kept the economy growing (Kurth, 34). Because of its historical development of a significant middle class, the United States has been in a position traditionally to maintain a high level of education for elite and middle-sector groups. After World War II more middle-sector groups benefited from the G.I. Bill for American veterans.

In the mid-1960s, ethnic Americans began to enter U.S. colleges and universities because of the civil rights momentum in the U.S. The Vietnam War galvanized students, particularly as they were of military age and were being drafted by the Selective Service Board. While China's and Mexico's political culture was extremely weak in terms of effective citizen participation and dissent, the U.S. political culture was extremely well developed and effective from the standpoint of citizen participation. Both Almond and Powell believe that "a political culture is a particular distribution of political attitudes, values, feelings, information, and skill that provide the psychological environment within which a political system operates." (Ranney 569). They believe "political culture is one of the most important elements in the political system" (Ranney 569). Unlike China and Mexico, the United States has a high degree of participation in its political system.* Besides voting, its citizens can serve in political office, and donate to their chosen candidates, causes, and parties of their choice. In

---

* In the U.S. 2020 elections, there was a 62% voting participation, the largest ever, but 38% didn't turn out at the polls.

China and Mexico, the political authorities manipulate and control who will be able to participate, although there is greater access to the system in Mexico today. The political system in the U.S. allows for dissent or alternative views and criticism as its citizens have the freedom to boycott, sign petitions, and participate in demonstrations (Ranney).

Today, in the modern 2020s, Mexico is faced with dangerous and fatal killings due to the out-of-control drug cartel violence and also the dangerous and violent murders of journalists that rock the nation. That creates instability and fear in Mexican society. In China and Mexico, both authoritarian nations, the student movements were extremely threatening and caused the authorities to suppress their movement because they felt intimidated and threatened by them. The use of the media in China and Mexico was controlled by the government, and after the Spring Uprising in 1989 and the Student Massacre in 1968, the news of these tragic events was blacked out by the governments. In Mexico, the government was successful in its attempt to cover up its attack on students. In China, the CCP also blacked out and tried to cover up the massacre, but they were unsuccessful as communications via the worldwide Internet could not be blocked. In the United States, the media and communications industry played a crucial role as coverage of the Vietnam War was presented daily and showed the U.S. casualties of the American troops on television. The free press or news media told the story of the protests and recorded interviews on the growing anti-war movement. In comparison, the student movements in each nation, China, Mexico, and the United States, were led by passionate student leaders who believed deeply in their cause. Relying on large numbers, each movement used its followers to fill the streets to protest in organized marches and political rallies to communicate their demands.

Both China and Mexico were extremely weakened and curtailed as they were unable to develop national support from labor unions, churches, and professional associations, which were controlled by their governments. However, in the United States, national associations were involved as a major part of the movement. The primary make-up of student movement supporters and leaders in China and Mexico were elite and middle-class members, who attended university, technical, and science academies. In the United States, the student movement included elite, middle, and lower-class members, who attended universities and colleges. In China and Mexico, both movements began initially as protests against government corruption but then advanced to demands for democracy in their political system. Except for the United States, which had a liberal democracy with well-developed institutions and government, their demand was to end the Vietnam War and to scale back the power of the FBI and the CIA. Each student movement was involved in a political struggle against its government leaders. In China, it was Deng Xiaoping, and in Mexico, it was Gustavo Diaz Ordaz who ordered the crackdown on students which led to the crushing of student dissident movements. In the United States, it was Presidents Lyndon B. Johnson and Richard M. Nixon who exerted great authority to expand the war which brought increasing opposition and student protest and unrest. Many of the movements' students suffered persecution, police beatings, and death, primarily in China and Mexico, and to a lesser extent in the U.S. The students suffered for their passionate cause and paid the ultimate price with their lives for freedom. We must not forget their ultimate sacrifice!

The United States Review Questions

REVIEW QUESTIONS FOR DISCUSSION AND ANALYSIS

1. Discuss the level of checks and balances and how the American political system encouraged higher levels of tolerance and critical dissent.

2. How did the American student Anti-War Movement alter National politics using the Voting Rights Act of 1971 and The Selective Service Board Draft System?

3. What was the military policy of President Lyndon Baines Johnson called The Gulf of Tonkin Resolution? How did it affect the Vietnam War?

4. What was the common complaint of the draft system of African American and Mexican American youth?

5. Discuss the role and impact of Pentagon specialist, Daniel Ellsberg.

6. Identify the analysis of political scientist Samuel P. Huntington and what he believed was propelling student beliefs in their activism against the war.

7. Briefly describe the segments of the American population who joined the student Anti-war protest movement.

8. Briefly discuss the views of Nathan Glazer on the effectiveness of radical tactics.

9. How did the student anti-war movement leaders come to establish the university as a major focus in American politics?

10. Did the American student anti-war movement have the impact of changing internal domestic policy and external foreign policy?

11. According to Tom Wells, "The Vietnam War evoked a clash unprecedented in American affairs. Explain.

12. Identify how U.S. citizens expressed their unprecedented dissent against the Vietnam war.

13. What amendment gave the power of protest to the Anti-War Movement?

14. Was the United States student anti-war movement successful? Explain.

15. According to Almond and Powell, why is a nation's political culture an important factor for political representation?

16. Discuss the importance of media and communications and how they played a key factor as coverage during the Vietnam War.

17. What reasons are listed to claim that the student anti-war movement in the United States was the most successful?

18. What can we learn from student dissident movements? How much do students play a significant role in shaping domestic and international policy?

Conclusion

A final analysis indicates that in Mexico the student movement did not have any significant impact on domestic and international relations. The oppressive political system of the government through the PRI effectively contained and eliminated student dissent. Mexican leaders pursued the development of economic policies for further modernization and stabilization of its relations with the United States. The dissident movement in Mexico was primarily a student and intellectual movement that was unable to develop subnational support as the government-controlled significant unions and associations, thereby limiting its influence. In China, the dissident movement had a small base of support, but it was also very limited and controlled by the dominance of the Chinese Communist Party.

The student movement in China contained more elements of the middle sector than Mexico's movement, but still remained relatively insignificant. The Chinese dissident movement did produce a large impact on domestic and international policy. The crisis at Tiananmen Square caused Deng's political leadership to pursue the economic policies of modernization to expand capitalist strategies to meet the needs of the middle and lower sectors of society and overcome negative publicity and world opinion. The student movements of both Mexico and China brought attention and awareness to their societies and showed that their political systems, however, different, were unable to engage in any open democratic dialogue or develop civic trust and participation among their citizens. The student movement in the U.S. was most successful in its attempts to make a significant impact on its government. Because of America's liberal traditions and constitution, the student movement was allowed to protest vocally and so became a central part of the anti-war movement. Even as the government attempted to discredit leaders opposed to the war, the peace advocates and radicals produced a definite impact on domestic and international policy. Their impact was so strong that U.S. defense institutions were weakened, thus causing U.S. foreign policies to be questioned and eventually altered. They directly influenced the decision to end the Vietnam War, which was the most pressing political debate in America at that time.

In 1968 Mexico's economic and international relationships were extremely crucial for Mexico since the country needed stable relations with the U.S. in order to maintain economic ties and trade with the U.S. The Cuban Revolution (1959) added great tension to U.S. policy in Latin America as Cuba also maintained ties to the Soviet Union. Mexico, while friends to the U.S., also supported the right of Cuba's self-determination and had to continue to keep a balance between its own sovereignty and its economic relations with the U.S.

The Cold War and the Vietnam War both set up adversarial relations with the Soviet Union and China as they were Communist nations and were locked in the bipolar structure between the U.S. and the Soviet Union. In the nuclear arms race, the U.S. was attempting through its policies to contain the Communist threat in Europe, Asia, and Latin America. They believed that Communism could also spread to Mexico, and they were concerned because of the strong criticism of U.S. imperialism from student leaders in Mexico. Therefore, the U.S. had CIA operatives monitoring the student movement in Mexico. Significant political transformations began to evolve, nearing the post-Cold War period of 1989. Great changes were coming to Eastern Europe as a Solidarity Movement was challenging the authority of the Communist government in Poland.

Hungary, Czechoslovakia, and Romania were also experiencing great difficulty in their Communist economic and political systems and were experiencing great instability in their governance system. The Soviet Union under Mikhail Gorbachev was attempting to reform the economic and political system through Perestroika (restructuring the economic system) and Glasnost (open government). In his move, he attempted to restructure the Soviet Union's decaying and disintegrating system. These dramatic events of great change and instability were signaling the decline and disintegration of the Soviet Empire and caused grave concern in China.

Democratization had already come to Portugal and also to parts of Latin America, and Chinese leaders were very nervous watching these developments. They were determined to prevent any such changes from coming to China. China had taken a bold move to modernize its economy and enter the global market, and the country had already seen changes in its society and desired to control these powerful forces of potential upheaval. The student movement in China was focused on bringing democracy to China. Their emphasis was on changing the political system. They were in agreement with the economic policies of modernization in 1989, and they desired to continue to bring wealth to all citizens. The political leadership of the CCP did not want to accelerate the forces of modernization so rapidly, in order to be better able to control social and economic changes. They were reluctant to increase economic modernization, but after the uprising and the international political fallout, they resumed their economic policies of modernization as a means of placating their citizens and moving China forward economically. The Mexican student movement was primarily devoted to democracy and was also concerned over poverty in their country. The student movement found little support, and the government saw them merely as an obstacle needing to be removed so they could continue their policies of economic development and modernization.

In both China and Mexico, the lack of well-developed institutions, civil societies, political culture, and heavy control of all major national associations insured the government's efforts to exercise total power effectively over these movements in order to eliminate them. What the student movements did, however, through their protests was to start the process of democratization. Today, Mexico is on the path of developing important institutions, civic bodies, and media, which will, in time, bring greater democracy to the country.[25] Mexican journalists killed added to the media death toll by Lizbeth Diaz and Kylie Madry according to Reuters news source on October 3, 2022, reporting 13 murders of journalists in 2022. This is shocking and unprecedented. Violence against the press has gone up 85% from President Andres Manuel Lopez Obrador's administration.

In China this process will also occur as the Mao generation of leadership will be replaced by The Tiananmen Square generation of student leaders who survived. In the United States, the student movement was also political and was very successful in bringing about political change in its domestic and foreign policy because it was aided by well-developed political institutions and government, which had an effective checks and balances system and a strong participatory society and political culture that expressed dramatically their views and intentions to oppose their own political leaders to bring to an end the Vietnam War. Thus, in China, the democracy movement failed as its political system and institutions did not allow dissent or compromise. Political authorities held on to power and ended the protest with state violence. Similarly, in Mexico, the democratic movement ended likewise with state violence as their leaders were not able to coopt the dissidents effectively and could not permit them to gain influence and dictate a change in their political system. In the United States, the anti-war movement was significant and was the only movement to alter U.S. domestic and international policy. The U.S. political system was the only democratic system, and it had a high degree of political development where criticism and protest were tolerated.

In 2020, the United States faced critical danger from former president Trump and his followers who threatened the overthrow of the Presidential election when the winner Joe Biden was elected president of the United States. Former president Donald J. Trump and his allies supported the anti-democratic effort to stop the electoral process in his failed January 6, 2021 insurrection! This action is a violation of the U.S. Constitution and is now being investigated thoroughly by the 1/6 Committee led by Bennie Gordon Thompson U.S. representative for Mississippi's 2nd Congressional District since 1992. Attorney General Merrick Garland and the Department of Justice have vowed in a speech on the anniversary of January 6 that all persons regardless of how high their positions maybe will be held accountable! "No one is above the law," they say!

History will conclude that from evidence gathered by the January 6, 2021 panel, former president Donald J. Trump violated his oath and on purpose incited the insurrection of January 6 with his fiery speech of betrayal of the U.S. Constitution and made efforts to overturn the electoral process, which concluded by proclaiming presidential candidate Joe Biden as the winner of the 2020 presidential election and new president of the country and defeating a traitor and dictator in his lust for power. At the time of writing, the 1/6 Committee currently conducting the investigation is compiling important evidence which will leave it up to the Department of Justice to take up charges of constitutional violations and proceed with indictments.

Notes

[1] Deng Xiaoping came to power in 1978 as a winner (Kornberg and Faust) of a power struggle within the Communist Party and won out over the Gang of Four, principally the widow of Mao, Jiang Qing.

[2] My interpretation of Western cultural influences would mean the social and cultural influences from the West that would impact Chinese traditional values, thoughts and customs in dress, food, music, and art. The reference to immoral conduct and crime refers to the growing problem of pornography, which could be attributed to modernization. Leaders of the CCP from its inception have sought to legitimize itself through mobilization of Chinese traditional values (Kornberg and Faust). "Some leaders are more oriented toward the open door policy, whereas others will seek to prevent further penetration of China's culture and traditions from the outside…" (Kornberg and Faust 3) These leaders were concerned "As consumer goods proliferated, and life-styles diversified. Of course, such phenomena as corruption, crime and pornography increased" (Womack and Townsend 410).

[3] The government was neither positive nor negative, i.e., petitions to grant amnesty to political prisoners (Womack and Townsend 426) were ignored, and students were not punished. Citizens were quite open at this point about expressing their grievances and disagreements about government, and students organized democracy salons where discussions on democracy were common (Almond).

[4] "The new emphasis on academic quality, higher education, and international openness transformed the educational world of the 1980s in China. To be sure the CCP and the CYL continued to occupy central institutional roles, and open challenges to authority were risky. But the requirement of ideological correctness became a more distant and intermittent influence on academic life"(Womack and Townsend 439).

[5] As economic problems escalated and as the government was unwilling to dialogue to find a solution at an early stage, the situation worsened and then

boiled to a point when military action was becoming inevitable (Salisbury).

[6] In the later 1970s and 1980s, a "wave of democracy" spread to Portugal and Latin America, thus ending decades of dictatorial, authoritarian rule and constituting a new phenomenon expanding societies on their road to basic freedoms.

[7] Many of these exceptional students at the universities were accomplished scholars, who commanded a strong influence in fields of physics, engineering, medical studies, electrical power, and science. However, students and professors represented only one percent of China, and at least one million supporters were backing the students. Supporters of the democracy movement numbered around one million (Kornberg and Faust).

[8] Protests started by Sunday June 4 hours after the massacre as well as protest demonstrations, which started nearly immediately.

[9] The modernization policies of Deng's administration created reduced state controls on economic activity and relaxed political tension. This allowed greater pursuit of profit among the populace and they sought to add new life style changes and more diversity in their lives. Decontrol and the new prosperity opened up society for more choices. The Tiananmen demonstrators were pressing for democracy, and at the bottom of society they demanded "That China's leaders acknowledge and guarantee the new diversity and freedom of society" (Womack and Townsend 410). It is my interpretation based on this information, that many in China supported the idea of reform and agreed with the demonstrators.

[10] Media sources were: Voice of America, the BBC World Service, and standard Internet services worldwide like AOL, Yahoo, and Hotmail. The educated elite and the middle elite had use of international chat rooms online and had instant access to email and traditional computer Internet services worldwide.

[11] "The brutal massacre in Beijing made many governments and international organizations adopt sanctions against China, and China's international trade and tourism dropped off precipitously (Womack and Townsend 409) But China was not to be ostracized very long, after six months the sanctions softened and Iraq's invasion of Kuwait called for China's cooperation in the United Nations (Womack and Townsend).

[12] "With the boosting of private enterprise and the winding down of the state sector, the Communist party has lost much of the control it once enjoyed over ordinary people's lives" (Miles).

[13] From an address Diaz Ordaz gave, he states "In every young man there is a substance generally pure, generous, idealistic," but he knew that the young were restless and unruly and felt by nature they were lawless and easily manipulated by "outside agitators." To think of them was to think of police (Krauze 655). Various sources discuss Díaz Ordaz's presidency and the events leading to the Tlatelolco Massacre, including The Tlatelolco Massacre. SpringerLink, https://link.springer.com/chapter/10.1007/978-1-349-12192-2_2 and Wikipedia, https://en.wikipedia.org/wiki/Gustavo_D%C3%ADaz_Ordaz.

[14] Sources I researched do not list the number of students and supporters killed, but there were 15,000 bullets expended. The government reported three casualty figures: first report—8, second report—18, and third report 43—killed. Others indicate 400 to several thousand unofficially.

[15] Student supporters included many science and philosophy departments and influential scholars from the National University. There were Catholics in the movement, PAN members, even priests; Faculty of Sciences, Faculty of Engineering, influential scholar Herberto Castillo and artist José Pepe Revueltos, and were going to the working class neighborhoods but the campuses were the main centers of the movement with only one teachers' coalition and one independent trade union.

[16] Further, the Vietnam War, which began in the early sixties and expanded to momentous proportions, absorbed the entire nation and came to reflect a great political divide as the country experienced a national mobilization of many segments of the population organized to pursue American leaders to end the military conflict in Vietnam and Southeast Asia (Valdez 7).

[17] UCB is the birthplace of the Free Speech Movement in 1964 (Sproul Plaza) that is considered to be the beginning of the student rebellion in this country from Nathan Glazer's article "Student Politics and the University" (The Atlantic Monthly, July 1969).

[18] Robert Putnam, a renowned political theorist, bases his research on civil society. He identifies the role and importance of civic trust and participation and affirms that these vital ingredients are important to the principles of democracy and democratization (Valdez 22).

[19] According to Leffler, 1999, "American officials began to think seriously about the nation's postwar security during 1943-1944. Military planners devised elaborate plans for an overseas base system." "Two strategic considerations influenced the development of an overseas base system. The first was the

need for defense in depth. Since attacks against the United States could only emanate from Europe and Asia..." (Leffler, 113).

[20] While we cannot know with certainty the number of Chicanos and Latinos killed in the Vietnam conflict, because of Pentagon record keeping practices during that period, we can point to the high percentage of Spanish surnames on the Vietnam Memorial in Washington, D.C. and to ample anecdotal evidence in every Chicano and Latino barrio in the nation. The example of activist-scholar Lea Ybarra of Chicano Studies, California State Fresno (1989) and author of *Too Many Heroes: The Oral History of Chicano VietNam Veterans*, is not an unique case. During the Vietnam War period, 18 of Dr. Ybarra's cousins served in the U.S. military.

[21] Most foreign policy initiatives were supported by both political partes, and the range of debate about alternatives was limited according to Lipsitz and Speak. "However, that picture changed drastically, as debate over foreign policy matters intensified" (Lipsitz and Speak 198). At the 1968 Democratic convention in Chicago control of the proceedings was very tight, and some delegates wanted a more open convention and an anti-Vietnam plank, as did protestors who were being set upon by police, "sometimes taunting police, sometimes set upon and beaten by police with little or no provocation" (Lipsitz and Speak 237).

[22] Both Presidents Johnson and Nixon utilized the C.I.A., F.B.I. and a newly developed counter insurgency agency called COINTELPRO established to find Communist links to the critics of the war.

[23] Four students were killed, and nine were wounded in 13 seconds. 61 shots were fired. Ten days later a disturbance occurred at Jackson State University in Jackson, Mississippi. On May 14, 1970, students threw bricks and bottles at passing white motorists. Two Blacks were killed, and twelve were wounded by State Police... (Report of the President's Commission on Campus Unrest, 1970).

[24] This analysis on S. L. Feuer also comes from John Valdez's Modern Latin American History Research Paper at a graduate seminar from the University San Diego, Fall 1995.

[25] Krauze makes reference to an important meeting among PRI, PAN, and PRD leaders in 1995 to expedite the transition to a true democracy (Krauze 795).

Works Cited

Acuna, Rodolfo. *Occupied America: A History of Chicanos.* Longman, 1981.

Almond, Gabriel A. *The Civic Culture: Political Attitudes and Democracy in Five Nations.* SAGE Publications, 1992.

Cornelius, Wayne, and Ann Craig. *The Mexican Political System in Transition.* Monograph Series 35, San Diego: University of California, Center for U.S.-Mexican Studies, 1991.

Encyclopedia Britannica, Inc. *The New Encyclopedia Britannica.* Vol. 7, 1986.

Feuer, L. S. *The Conflict of Generations: The Character and Significance of Student Movements.* Basic Books, New York, 1969.

Gifford, Rob. " Student division leads Tiananmen failure." *BBC News,*3 June 1999, http://news.bbc.co.uk/2/hi/special_report/1999/06/99/tiananmen_square/360042.stm

Glazer, Nathan. *Student Politics and the University.* The Atlantic Monthly, July 1969.

Huntington, Samuel P. *American Politics: The Promise of Disharmony. Harvard University Press,* 1981.

Kornberg, Judith F., and John R. Faust. *China in World Politics: Policies, Processes, Prospects.* Lynne Rienner Publishers, 1995.

Kurth, James. *The Political Economy of Defense: The Impact of the Military-Industrial Complex.* Harper & Row, 1972.

Krauze, Enrique. *Mexico, Biography of Power: A History of Modern Mexico, 1810-1996.* Harper Perennial, 1998.

Leffler, Melvyn P. *A Preponderance of Power: National Security, the Truman Administration, and the Cold War.* Stanford University Press, 1992.

Meyer, Michael C., William L. Sherman, and Susan M. Deeds. The Course of Mexican History. 7th ed., Oxford University Press, 2003.

Miles, James. "Tiananmen: The Birth of Economic Revolution." *BBC News*, 4 June 2000, news.bbc.co.uk/2/hi/special_report/1999/06/99/tiananmen_square/358399.stm

Paz, Octavio. "México: The Last Decade." *Is the Mexican Revolution Dead?*, edited by Stanley R. Ross, Temple University Press, 1975, p. 245.

---. *Posdata*. Siglo Veintiuno Editores, 1970, p. 38.

Ranney, Austin. *Governing: An Introduction to Political Science*. Prentice Hall, 1996.

Salisbury, Harrison E. *Tiananmen Diary: Thirteen Days in June*. Little, Brown, 1989.

Schultz, Stanley K., and William P. Schultz. *The Democratic Experience: A Short History of the United States*. 4th ed., McGraw-Hill, 1994.

Valdez, John. *Independent Studies Research Paper*. University San Diego. Fall 2001.

---. Modern Latin American History Research Paper. University of San Diego, Graduate Seminar, Fall 1995.

Womack, Brantly, and Carolyn L. Townsend. "China's Democratic Tradition." *China in World Politics: Policies Processes, Prospects*, by John R. Faust and Judith F. Kornberg, Lynne Rienner Publishers, 1995.

Ybarra, Lea. *Too Many Heroes: The Oral History of Chicano Vietnam Veterans*. California State University, Fresno, 1989.

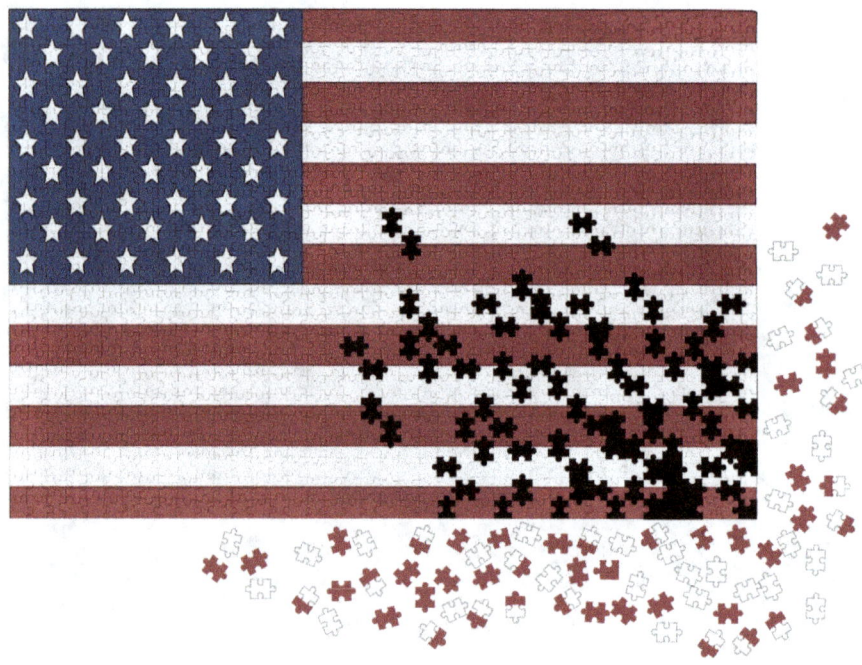

THIRD CASE STUDY

Multiculturalism in America and American Foreign Policy: Elements of Unification or Fragmentation?

John E. Valdez

THIRD CASE STUDY SUMMARY DEBATE:
PART ONE

Unification or Fragmentation: Multiculturalism in America and American Foreign Policy

UNIFICATION OR FRAGMENTATION?

According to respected political theorists like John Gerard Ruggie and Samuel P. Huntington, multiculturalism or ethnic diversity in the extreme can threaten American social and political values, create domestic instability, and has the potential to negatively impact American foreign policy. This case study investigates the hypothesis on militant multiculturalism to determine if this is an accurate perception and if this premise is valid. Also, the case study investigates whether a multicultural creed can be formulated that reflects the principles of multiculturalism if it is compatible or incompatible with the American Creed and if such a creed is incompatible with American foreign policy.

FRAGMENTATION

"'Cultural Wars' splinter the ideational project of American community into multiple, competing, and often presumed mutually hostile identities."

- Ruggie, <u>Winning the Peace</u>, 1996, p. 167

"At some point traditional American ideals-liberty, equality, individualism, and democracy may lose their appeal and join the ideals of racial inequality,

the divine right of kings, and the dictatorship of the proletariat on the ideological scrap heap of history."

- Huntington, <u>American Ideals vs. American Institutions</u>, 1982, p. 229

UNIFICATION

Multiculturalism and its movement: Hollinger sees signs that multiculturalism is creating more positive interactions toward a more harmonious relationship in our society. He "sees hope that this debate is circling back in search of new means for a stretching of a we."

- Hollinger, <u>Postethnic America</u>: Beyond Multiculturalism, 1994, p. 168

"It seems unlikely to me that cultural diversity and the challenge it poses will decrease during the new century. If anything, diversity seems likely to increase. if in the past, democratic countries have not always dealt with cultural diversity in ways consistent with democratic practices and values, can they, and will they, do better in the future?"

- Dahl, Robert, 1989. <u>On Democracy.</u>
New Haven and London: Yale University Press.

The Debate: Fragmentation? Influential political theorists express alarm that extreme multiculturalism and its militancy can negatively impact domestic and international American foreign policy as well as alter the American core principles of the American Creed: Liberty, Democracy, Equality, and Individualism.

The Challenge: Influential advocates and political theorists for multiculturalism refute these alarmists' claims and reaffirm that a multicultural society and creed invigorate diversity in American society and embrace the core principles of the American Creed rooted in greater diversity for all people striving for the American Dream.

Debate and Challenge: The Third Case Study will examine and debate the subject of multiculturalism in America to assess, in theory, if it can weaken or undo the core American principles of the American Creed, which is the American historical and political foundation of our nation. American theorists who are deeply concerned with ethnic and social movements are alarmed over the political activism of Civil Rights and Ethnic revitalization movements of the 1960s and 1970s and onward. Multicultural advocates and civil rights leaders believe that the growing ethnic revitalization movements championing social, cultural, and civil rights are an outgrowth of their desire for justice and self-determination, for a prosperous life with equality of opportunity for all. They are committed to the core American principles and to the promise of the spirit and truth of the American Creed, "E Pluribus Unum," out of many one, which elevates all Americans based on inclusion and which makes this beloved nation more prosperous, democratic and just.

What both Ruggie and Huntington seem to fear is a threat to American foreign policy and what can be seen as core values expressed in the American Creed. They fear that ethnic groups within America will threaten international policy with a shift in focus from international to domestic. Also, they fear a change in the American Creed.

American Creed Core Values: The Heart and Soul of America

What are the core values of the American Creed that shape American identity? Gunnar Myrdal in his important work of the 1940s titled: *An American Dilemma: The Negro Problem and Modern Democracy,* states that the values that imbue what he coined "The American Creed" form the core of American national identity and can be defined as liberty, equality of opportunity, democracy, and individualism. He believes that these ideals are the heart and soul of American values and are the principles that have shaped the political identity, character, and ideology of America since its inception. They continue to leave their legacy on American political culture, as well as to influence American foreign policy. The American Creed fosters the spirit of inclusivity.

AMERICAN CREED IDEALS

1. **LIBERTY.** Liberty does not mean just doing what one feels like doing. It means liberty comes with responsibility. Real liberty means using freedom in ways that humanely address "The Others" and every life's essential needs in order to survive.

2. **EQUALITY**. Equality means equality of opportunity, where each person is at a different point of consciousness and is so created equal innately but may not be consciously expressing(yet) a high degree of awareness.

3. **INDIVIDUALISM.** Individualism must be ethical and empathetic, expressive—not just narcissistic gratification of selfishness, especially at the expense of others. A person's character matters in contributing to a society and nation. Key features in promoting self-reliance and positive individualism is respect for others and self-development to cultivate the individual's gifts and talents for the greater good.

4. **DEMOCRACY.** Democracy must aim to express the will of the majority

"The People," not just the elites or powerful.

The shining principles can inspire and promote inclusive possibilities of hope and promise to the citizens of America. Unfortunately, the American promise of democratic equality, which is one of the foundations of the American Creed, has been historically denied to ethnic Americans through unfair political practices and policies which have deprived American ethnic citizens of their constitutional rights. In the contemporary political modern landscape, the movement of voter suppression by the GOP has spread to up to 18 states in the U.S. which focus on voter suppression. In 2021, new barriers were created in nineteen states that enacted thirty-four laws restricting access to voting. Obstacles to voting used are rules surrounding voter ID, mail voting, resource allocation at polling places, and voter roll maintenance unfortunately create significant problems and will seriously impact communities of the ethnic population unfairly. American citizens need to be prepared, informed, and vigilant in strategies to combat these voting assaults designed to de-power the American ethnic voter.

RUGGIE CORE OF FEARS

1. **Separatist politics**
2. **Culture Wars**
3. **View of foreign policy within a fragmented environment**
4. **Ethnic militant politics draws attention from International to Domestic concerns**

Ruggie has stated that separatist politics or the politics of separatism and dissent have created turmoil in American society, and have led to greater divisions within all groups. The fact he states this detracts from American policy abroad. He believes conflicts within society are not good for a stable foreign policy. Ruggie's greatest disdain for ethnic militant politics in America is that they are opportunistic, exaggerated, and only promote a false agenda giving just entitlements (Ruggie 167). Ruggie goes on to ask what kind of politics can be a viable foreign policy that can be shaped in this period of separatist policies.

HUNTINGTON CORE OF FEARS

1. Civil Rights movements of the 1960s and 1970s adversely affected government policy or American Foreign Policy

2. Ethnic movements within America weaken Foreign Policy
3. Immigration has the potential to alter negatively the American Creed
4. A challenge by ethnic groups is a challenge to American Identity - Resulting in negative changes to American ideas and ideals

Huntington's concern regarding ethnic militant groups is based on what he perceives as a negative impact of the Civil Rights movement and those ethnic groups protesting against the Vietnam War. As a result of these movements, the changes in government policy he believed adversely impacted the government, weakening foreign policy and contributing to what he believed was the demise of U.S. policy. Accordingly, Huntington believes, "the more culturally pluralistic the nation becomes, particularly if cultural pluralism encompasses linguistic pluralism, the more essential the political values of the creed become in defining what it is that Americans have in common. At some point, traditional American ideals—liberty, equality, individualism, democracy—may lose their appeal and join the ideas of racial inequality, the divine right of kings, and the dictatorship of the proletariat on the ideological scrap heap of history." He then goes on and contradicts himself by concluding: "There is, however, little to suggest that this will be a twentieth-century happening" (Huntington 229).

Huntington believes that the dissidents among ethnic/moralist groups in the US also lead to a weakening of the central government; curbing their power, thus shifting the focus from international to domestic concerns. This result, lessens the gap between American ideals and American institutions, resulting in the weakening of the perception of America abroad. Conversely, The "Creedal passion" period Huntington identifies as the major development in America is where the various movements' leaders have sought to narrow the gap between specific values and the institutions that define America's identity and the principle of equality. As a result, Huntington fears that the focus on domestic concerns creates a perceived weakness of America abroad, as citizens are able to restructure policies of the government, shifting attention away from foreign to more domestic concerns. Huntington also has a fear of Latin immigration and has been quoted as saying: "Latin immigration could reinforce the central role of the American Creed both as a way of legitimizing claims to political, economic and social equality and also as the indispensable element in defining national identity"(Huntington 229).

A current source of new world immigration has come about from the conflict from Vladimir Putin's war on Ukraine, where Russia invaded and attacked Ukraine on February 24, 2022. This unprovoked war of aggression by Putin has forced 13 million people to leave their homes according to the United Nations. Almost five million have left for nearby countries and eight million are believed to be displaced inside of Ukraine due to the invasion.

According to news sources, nearly 6,000 Ukrainians have been approved to enter the U.S. based on President Biden's administrative website. President Biden's goal is to bring 100,000 Ukrainians fleeing the war to the U.S. according to NBC News. More than 3.2 million people have crossed the border from Ukraine to Poland since February 24, 2022.

OTHER FEARS

Katznelson & Kesselman

> "The increasing fragmentation and conflict within American society, identified as the process of 'Balkanization' or 'atomization.' Katznelson & Kesselman fear fragmentation of American identity that ultimately will affect American economic and political arrangements.

Schlesinger, Jr.

> "Cult of Ethnicity" today's new ethnics are obstructing the past assimilation & integration of American identity which implies that it could impact domestic solidarity and create instability in leadership in American foreign policy. Schlesinger comments that today throughout the world there are great ethnic tensions that threaten the nations of the world. I quote, **"On every side, today ethnicity is breaking up nations. The Soviet Union, India, Yugoslavia, and Ethiopia are all in crisis. Ethnic tensions disturb and divide Sri Lanka, Burma, Indonesia, Iraq, Cyprus, Nigeria, Angola, Lebanon, Guyana, Trinidad—you name it. Even nations as stable and civilized as Britain, and France, Belgium and Spain face growing ethnic troubles. Is there any large multiethnic state that can be made to work?"** (Schlesinger 129).

According to Schlesinger Jr's comment, great instability has the potential to threaten the nations of the world. However, it is possible that such comments are overly exaggerated and generally not the case. For example, the history of immigration to the United States has always resulted in positive gains for new immigrants and has always served key interests in the economy of this country. Historically Mexican immigration to the United States has greatly benefited the country in WWII and Korean War, immensely.

In the book called *Let Us Dream*, Pope Francis writes that immigrants are seeking a "path to a better future." Pope Francis writes that the new immigrants are seeking safety from violence, corruption, and abuse from corrupt officials and notorious gangs found in Central America. In time immigrants find ways to overcome obstacles as they acclimate and find a better future for themselves and their families through hard work and support from their communities and gatekeepers.

On a personal note, my own father as a youth, Eduardo Valdez, came to the United States from Mexico during the Mexican Revolution from 1910 to 1929. As a teenage youth, he was conscripted to join the Mexican military and maybe due to his young age, he became a chauffeur to the Mexican General at the time. My father told me that the general was killed in a battle and that is when he left the army. He crossed the border and arrived to Arizona, later joined the U.S. military, and prepared to fight for the United States. He received training at Fort Huachuca in Arizona to be sent to Europe in 1918 during World War I. Fortunately, he was not sent as WWI ended in November 11 of 1918.

Additionally, my mother Justina Garcia, before she got married to my father, came to San Diego with mother Josefa Garcia and settled in Lemon Grove, California. There she met my father and got married on Feast Day of Lady of Guadalupe on December 12, 1931 in St. Martin's Catholic Church, La Mesa, California. Her uncle Tio Capitan Ignacio Beltan was killed during the Revolution. He was my mother's benefactor and provided for her education at a Catholic convent in Mazatlán, Sinaloa in Mexico until he was killed as she finished second grade. Both my father and mother sought safety and refuge. They both were able to pursue a new life and seek God, family and work to build their family dreams. Personally, I thank God for that!

Today, due to unfortunate circumstances, numerous nations have come to the United States seeking safety, a better way of life, and security for themselves and their families. Immigrants arrive as a result of displacement due to threats that affect their well-being such as threats of violence, political and social persecution, and problems due to a lack of economic livelihoods and poor sustainability where they cannot provide for their families. Immigrants follow the call of self-preservation. Currently, people from other nations seeking self-preservation, safety, and protection of themselves and their families arrive to the United States with hope and gratitude in their hearts and a large appreciation of this nation for the safety and great opportunities it offers to make a dignified life. Many come from Afghanistan, Asia, Africa, Central America regions, Iran, Mexico, Serbia, Syria, and, since February 2022, many more from Ukraine due to Russia's attack and invasion. New immigrants arrive to the United States fleeing from their countries due to terrible actions such as the invasion of Ukraine as a consequence of the actions of Vladimir Putin which has devastated that country and their innocent civilians who have been victimized by the brutal war occupation, torture, and killings of people. The United States is a symbol of justice and humanity, especially for immigrants coming from distinct and varied nations. It's important to never forget that this is a nation of immigrants and that over the decades these same immigrants have been the contributors to building the backbone of America.

John Valdez's parents Justina Garcia and Eduardo Valdez wedding on December 12, 1931 at St. Martin's Catholic Church, La Mesa, CA.

Wedding attendants top right side: Pascual Beltran, Candelaria Beltran and Maria Luisa Beltran. Young children on left unknown by the author.

John Valdez family photo archive.

THE ENDURANCE OF AMERICAN IDEALS

1. American Creed
2. Permanence
3. Embeddedness
4. Resilience
5. Reinvented & Adapted

The ideals expressed in the American Creed are founded on principles of equality, liberty, democracy, and individualism. These landmark principles along with the Constitution and Bill of Rights empower newcomers to seek their civil liberties and redress. Rather than seeing ethnic groups that actively pursue justice and self-determination as efforts undermining American foreign relations, they could be seen as groups that consistently re-awaken American ideals in the pursuit of justice. Many new immigrants are not centrally involved in any major political processes or policies. They are greatly concerned about their survival in the new country, adjusting to the new language and culture, as well as establishing economic stability. New immigrants have strong family and religious values and exhibit conformity to majority norms or aspire to middle-class values in American society.

Huntington's hypothesis that the new wave of immigrants could alter the balance of the American Creed lacks evidence, and in fact, shows just the opposite. The new immigrants, while keeping many of their cultural traditions, religions, and family customs, overwhelmingly adhere to the sanctity of the American Creed and readily adopt its principles as part of their identity. Even Huntington identifies American ideals as values easily adapted, **"American ideals and values have their origins in the 17th and 18th centuries; they have a "tremendous persistence and resiliency in the 20th century. The ideals and values have been easily adapted to the needs of successive generations" (Huntington 228).** This book provides case studies of newly naturalized Americans and their reflections on their new citizenship status, their great embrace, and their love of America as newfound citizens.

2050 U.S. Latino Polulation statistic. By 2050, Hispanics will exceed 100 million P.I. from *Right Before our Eyes Latino Past, Present and Future* by Robert Montemayor with Henry Mendoza 2004 by Tomás Rivera Policy Institute published by Scholargy Publishing, Tempe, AZ.

REFUTING THE FEARS ACCORDING TO RUGGIE

1. Sensationalized statements
   - Alarmist
   - Cause great unease
2. Assertions lack validity
3. Admit the unlikelihood of events occurring

Although Ruggie has used the term "Culture Wars" with negative connotations, he also indicates that cultural conflicts have decreased significantly and have become less threatening to American domestic relations in the U.S., he says: **"It is somewhat reassuring then, to recall that these cultural conflicts are not nearly as severe as earlier ones in this century have been. In addition, there are also theoretical reasons and survey data to suggest that considerably more common ground exists than has been supposed in these debates" (Ruggie 167).** Huntington addresses the possibility that the newest wave of immigrants from Mexico, Central, and South America has the potential to alter the character of the American Creed. However, Huntington also says that this change is not likely to occur and that the American Creed has great "tremendous resilience in American tradition, identity, and value for today and the future." Further, although Schlesinger tries to analyze ethnic tensions in the world by asserting that any one of those conflicts can be applied to situations comparable to the U.S., his generic comparisons of ethnic rivalries in Yugoslavia, and the concept of 'ethnic cleansing' of non-Serbians; or even nations as stable as Britain, France, and Belgium with their ethnic troubles cannot be automatically applied to U.S. ethnic tensions. Tensions are part of everyday life and are impacted by the forces of modernization and urbanization. Tensions developed in a country are to a great extent unique to that country. Ethnic tensions will always exist, and each one is unique and distinct to that region. However, to apply the problems of other regions generically and then conclude that these same tensions exist in the United States is not the best way of understanding the nature of these tensions. The ethnic tensions of other regions of the world are rooted in different social, economic, and unique political, historical realities. In the United States, ethnic tensions dissipate as immigrants increase their social and economic stability over time and acclimate to the American culture and system. As newcomers arrive to the United States culture and society, they achieve and learn to navigate their new surroundings and find a new sense of place and hope.

Katznelson and Kesselman go on to say that the threat of fragmentation to American identity was not jeopardized, "For example, during the entire period, no major movement or political party challenged in a sustained way the basic legitimacy of American economic and political arrangements. Furthermore, although social movements like the women's movement, black militants, and environmental activists achieved significant changes, American corporate capitalism remained intact" (Katznelson and Kesselman 106).

TRENDS IN THE 21ST CENTURY: EMERGING SIGNS OF A GREATER MULTICULTURAL SOCIETY EMANATING FROM THE CULTURAL SOCIAL INTERACTIONS AND EXPERIENCES OF CULTURAL DEMOCRACY

1. Multiculturalism is creating more positive interaction
   - More harmonious relationships in American society
   - A deeper understanding of what it means to be an American
2. Ethnic Leadership Today
   - Politics of confrontation have passed to the standard politics of accommodation
   - Key concern: Is equal opportunity being served?
3. New engagement: American ethnic groups pursue civil & social justice
4. Latinos are the largest ethnic group critical to dominant political parties
5. Debate on multiculturalism reflects "cognitive dissonance" between America's ideals & institutions
   - Debate between anti-multiculturalists & multiculturalists
     - Multiculturalists advocate cultural democracy

HOLLINGER SEES HOPE POSTETHNIC AMERICA THE STRETCHING OF "WE THE PEOPLE"

Historian David Hollinger, an analyst of multiculturalism and its movement, sees signs that multiculturalism is creating more positive interaction toward a more harmonious relationship in American Society and he comments, that he "sees hope that this debate is circling back in search of a new means for a stretching of a we" (Hollinger 168). Hollinger's brilliant perception of the **"We The People"** in America and the importance of "We" as a representation of unity, destiny, and a survival tool for a better and greater U.S. nation to meet a future within hope and courage as Americans.

The activism of ethnic Americans in dissent reflects a healthy political culture in pursuit of democracy in American society. The politics of confrontation have passed to the standard of politics of accommodation where domestic and international interests become central to ethnic leadership as political leaders. With special interests that relate to the constituents to ensure equality is being served to all. True democratic development and democracy at home will most likely overlap in American foreign policy which matters to a greater degree. The rise of ethnic revitalization movements has passed through this period of conflict and has become more accommodational and less militant.

AMERICAN ETHNIC GROUPS SEEKING CIVIC & SOCIAL JUSTICE

Today, taking place in the United States is a new engagement in which American ethnics are pursuing civic and social justice in all realms of life in accordance with American principles of democracy and the American Creed. This greater involvement indicates a positive growing civic character and identity that leans toward Hollinger's view of building a civic nation that will spread to all its citizens. Also, Ruggie tells of a California research project that analyzed attitudes of Blacks and Hispanics as "the American sense of identity remains a relative bedrock that could provide support for diverse foreign policy positions"(Ruggie 169). The research report concludes that ethnic-American respondents have a strong attachment to Lockean principles of The American Creed, support the General American foreign policies that constitute American interests, and that the American sense of self as a nation remains relatively intact. John Locke, the initiator of the Age of the Enlightenment in England and France, advocated for the principles of inclusivity in society which were: Liberty, Democracy, Equality, and Individualism.

The Latino population is now numerically the dominant ethnic group and is becoming more crucial to the dominant political parties in the U.S. The leadership of the Democratic and Republican parties in order to exercise a stable and unified American foreign policy will need to garner votes from these constituents and will need to develop a strategy that addresses their issues and needs.

Also, the debate on multiculturalism or diversity in America is a historical and cultural reality and reflects another "cognitive dissonance" as it positions two distinct concepts: one which proclaims diversity is our strength, and the opposite concept that proclaims diversity is the undoing of our core values and identity as Americans. The debate on multiculturalism in America is consistent as being an underlying pressure that exists and surfaces periodically in the social life of Americans.

The 20th-century movement of American ethnic groups and other civil rights groups of today is championing the principle of democracy in the political culture as the bridge to transform American society by embracing the growing multicultural aspects of ethnic Americans to the principle of democratic expressions towards stretching the inclusive norm of the "we" which blends with the fabric of cultural democracy. This concept and principle is blended and recognizes the unique, positive, and enriching aspects of the ever-expanding culture of American ethnic groups in the diverse American society and culture that adds to their rich heritage.

Unfortunately, because of former president Donald J. Trump's actions to call for the storming of the capitol on January 6, 2021, and to stop the electoral process to ratify Joe Biden's presidential victory, the U.S. has come to a near collapse of its democracy. The U.S. is greatly divided politically and has become a nation polarized. This great divide persists as the nation divides in Blue and Red states and not the United States of America as described by former president, Barack Obama. Instead of acting as one as referenced by Barack Obama, it's now a divided and fractured nation. This nation is being overcome by extreme supporters of Trump and by the voices of white supremacists and racists who are emboldened by Trump and his allies who continue to persist in the "Big Lie" that the 2020 presidential election was "stolen." This loss of democratic equilibrium for this country based on political division among U.S. Congressional leaders has threatened its historic balance as a democratic nation. The citizens of the United States must find a way, and the political leaders in the U.S. Congress must put the nation first to restore the democratic principles and protect all members of American society. The need for reconciliation is great, and now is the time to begin the process to strengthen this nation as a more inclusive, multi-ethnic democracy.

On June 16, 1858, a candidate for the U.S. Senate delivered the address to the Republican members in the House of Representatives. In his introduction, Abraham Lincoln said, "A house divided against itself cannot stand." These famous and powerful words come from Jesus and are recorded in all three synoptic gospels of Matthew, Mark, and Luke. This is an eternal truth that applies to this nation today and forever!

Mark 3:25

²⁵*If a house is divided against itself, that house cannot stand.*

Matthew 12:22-28

²²*Then they brought him a demon-possessed man who was blind and mute, and Jesus healed him, so that he could both talk and see.* ²³*All the people were astonished and said, "Could this be the Son of David?* ²⁴*But when the Pharisees heard this, they said, "It is only by Beelzebul, the prince of demons, that this fellow drives out demons." * ²⁵*Jesus knew their thoughts and said to them, "Every kingdom divided against itself will be ruined, and every city or household divided against itself will not stand."* ²⁶*If Satan drives out Satan, he is divided against himself. How then can his kingdom stand?* ²⁷*And if I drive out demons by Beelzebul, by whom do your people drive them out? So then, they will be your judges.* ²⁸*But if it is by the Spirit of God that I drive out demons, then the kingdom of God has come upon you.*

Luke 11:14-23

¹⁴*Now he was casting out a demon that was mute. When the demon had gone out, the mute man spoke, and the people marveled.* ¹⁵*But some of them said, "He casts out demons by Beelzebul, the prince of demons,"* ¹⁶*while others, to test him, kept seeking from him a sign from heaven.* ¹⁷*But he, knowing their thoughts, said to them, "Every kingdom divided against itself is laid waste, and a divided household falls.* ¹⁸*And if Satan also is divided against himself, how will his kingdom stand? For you say that I cast out demons by Beelzebul.* ¹⁹*And if I cast out demons by Beelzebul, by whom do your sons cast them out? Therefore, they will be your judges.* ²⁰*But if it is by the finger of God that I cast out demons, then the kingdom of God has come upon you.* ²¹*When a strong man, fully armed, guards his own palace, his goods are safe;* ²²*but when one stronger than he attacks him and overcomes him, he takes away his armor in which he trusted and divides his spoil.* ²³*Whoever is not with me is against me, and whoever does not gather with me scatters.*

John 17:20-21

²⁰*My prayer is not for them alone. I pray also for those who will believe in me through their message,* ²¹*that all of them may be one, Father, just*

as you are in me and I am in you. May they also be in us so that the world may believe that you have sent me.

Paul GaLations 5:15
[15]*If you bite and devour each other, watch out or you will be destroyed by each other.*

REALISTIC VIEWS OF MULTICULTURAL SOCIETIES

- Ethnic Americans score high on the attitudinal survey
- Ethnic Americans remain focused on domestic issues - however, lack strong support for ideological issues like multilateralism

The survey referenced by Ruggie also indicates that while the American sense of self as a nation remains, relatively intact, and that a major interest in political ideals of egalitarianism, as well as a fundamental sense of the United States' role in the arena of international relations, remain relatively high, but not their top priority. Like all societies, domestic interests that relate to their social and economic livelihoods, such as employment, education, immigration, and facing crime and violence will always be given priority. Studies show immigrants have always sought to be part of the American identity, and their attitudes have been ones of inclusion rather than separation. This may explain their lack of ideological support for multilateralism and more interest in their social needs based on domestic concerns and focus.

THE FUTURE OF DEMOCRACY IN AMERICA ACCORDING TO DAHL'S THEORY IN THE 21ST CENTURY.

Robert A. Dahl, an eminent scholar and distinguished visionary on democratic theories, outlines a theoretical framework that arises from the positive involvement and participation of its citizens in American politics.

1. **Dahl's theory on Democracy's transformation**
2. **Large-scale citizenship participation in the decision-making process**
3. **The political system will broaden**
4. **Ordinary citizens play a greater role.** Citizens will be empowered in the post-industrial period towards cultural democracy supported by organizational shifts:

- dominance to partnership;
- departmentalization to intersection, and
- segregation to pluralism; and finally,
- exclusion to cultural democracy

THREE MAJOR POLITICAL TRANSFORMATIONS

Dahl identifies three major political transformations. The first was in the 5th BCE, the second was in the 17th century. The third, according to Dahl, will be in the 21st century where the change from a guardianship model of government to large-scale citizenship participation in decision-making processes, will create a society where governing will take place from the bottom up. Further, according to Romo and Salerno, community-inspired civic participation and citizenship at all levels will contribute to bridging the gap between American ideals and institutions and the political leaders and informed citizens in a cultural democratic environment in the 21st century. Ordinary citizens will play a greater role according to Dahl's hypothesis, where citizens will be empowered in the post-industrial period towards cultural democracy supported by organizational changes, which will be influenced by shifts from 1- dominance to partnership, 2 - departmentalization to intersection, and 3 - segregation to pluralism; and finally, 4 - exclusion to cultural democracy.

If Dahl's hypothesis comes to be realized, the political system would be broadened, and greater input from society would allow for more input in the arena of American foreign policy as well.

THE AMERICAN CREED IN THE 21ST CENTURY WILL PROMOTE GREATER CIVIL PARTICIPATION AND WILL ALIGN WITH 'EQUAL OPPORTUNITY FOR ALL'

Total citizenry sectors and equality of opportunity for all.

1. Civic participation of all citizens involving all sectors of U.S. society
2. Political system broadened
3. Equality increased
4. Shift toward greater involvement
   - Narrows the gap between ideals & institutions
   - Greater equality evolves bringing greater stability to American Creed

CONCLUSION OF PART ONE: "WE THE PEOPLE"

If Dahl's hypothesis becomes a reality, the opportunity exists for an American foreign policy that would reflect a broader section of American society and represent fundamental changes moving from the elite to the broader-based total citizenry sectors of American society. In summary, it is possible that among the American Creed principles, particularly at this time in our history, it is the principle of equality of opportunity that speaks to the social and political needs of this nation, especially among American ethnic groups. The cultural democracy or Multicultural Creed also speaks of the importance of equality of opportunity for all. Therefore, they are mutually the same in this respect; except that multiculturalists include respect for ethnic and linguistic differences. Fortified with this philosophy, ethnic and social tensions will continue to exist, especially among radical conservatives, but if cultural democracy is strengthened, the domestic and international interests will also be integrated and grounded, and the institutions and policies will reflect greater equality which will bring benefit to the international arena and in American foreign policy.

The shape and form of multiculturalism creatively shape their weaving into the American fabric of identity and culture. Multiculturalism can fortify, strengthen, and unify this nation to fulfill the American spirit of E Pluribus Unum ("Out of many, one"). This is a sacred heritage that has evolved throughout America and has contributed to the heritage of multiculturalism. This is the E Pluribus Unum moment to acknowledge the rich diversity and lead to the new American Revolution to affirm that this is a nation of "we the people" as eloquently expressed by President Lyndon Johnson "not merely a nation but a nation of nations."

The new, multicultural E Pluribus Unum in the United States embodies and resonates in a unique American fabric that is enthusiastically inclusive and rich in diversity of all ethnic cultures. *Amen.*

Multiculturalism Today is an American Manifestation of Greatness and Uniqueness

MULTICULTURALISM TODAY AND FUTURE

Multiculturalism today in America is altering the American landscape and creating a new and unique cultural fabric that is vibrant, energetic, and rich in social and cultural diversity. Today, numerous immigrant groups from all parts of the world have arrived to make America their new homeland. Historically, American Ethnic groups have been here in America since the 17th century as Africans were enslaved and forced into the system of slavery to create wealth for their owners. Native Americans were driven off their native lands, exterminated, and forced to live on desolated reservations. In the war with The United States, the Mexican people were subject to the Treaty of Guadalupe Hidalgo, which ended the war in 1848, and were given the choice to remain as U.S. citizens. Their lives and future were difficult and many times conflictive as they were treated as second-class citizens. Chinese men were recruited to labor in the building of the railroad in California and in agriculture as well and met with persecution and violence in frontier societies. Japanese people also came to America to labor primarily in Agriculture and worked in the fishing industry in San Diego, California.

Joining these groups were the Filipino men, who also labored in the agricultural fields of California. Also, Indians from India joined to labor in the fields of agriculture in California. In the early 20th century, the Puerto Ricans joined the labor force in the U.S. Then in 1959 during the Cold War, Cubans fleeing the rise of Fidel Castro and the new regime, fled to the U.S. and were granted refuge by President Nixon and protected by American foreign policy of the U.S. along with Cubans and many others through immigration from all parts of South America. Because of wars, many others from the Middle East have come to our shores from Iraq, Afghanistan, Syria, and Iran. The historical fabric of multiculturalism, beginning from the 17th century to the present day, is deeply rooted in U.S. history, culture, and language and layered throughtout the regions of the U.S. and connected to the development and progress of the U.S. economy and is contributing to defending the interests of the U.S. during armed conflicts.

This historical connection of the varied ethnic groups of America who stand with pride in their historical service in all military branches of the U.S. Only during the Vietnam War did a youthful generation of student leaders raise a significant outcry and protest against military service in an unpopular war. Only then was there resistance to military service.

The U.S. military service and tradition is ever strong and valiant. Men and women serve this nation with honor, and many of them are ethnic Americans from many multicultural groups. In this greater and growing multicultural reality of America, it is important to return to the First People, the true Native Americans who were the first on the continent prior to European colonization: America's first people, who are still here teaching the importance of respect for Mother Earth, all the wisdom and love of nature. America must make a forgiveness claim to atone for its brutality and theft of their lands and for the forced slavery of the Africans brought to America to build the American Empire and also to recognize past historical abuses towards the people of México and other persecutions towards the Chinese. It must atone to the Japanese Americans for the Japanese Internment during WWII. With atonement, the people can forgive such historical crimes and be stronger and more honorable as a nation.

AMERICA'S SPIRITUAL AND MORAL ATONEMENT FOR HEALING

The question arises how is atonement possible at this time as a nation? Is atonement needed for this nation to restore amends to American ethnic groups who have suffered violence and brutality? Can 'we' as members of this great nation come to terms to understand how ethnic Americans have suffered great violence and that atonement for historical abuses and violent treatment towards American Native Indigenous people and African people subjected to slavery who were forced to be slaves in 1619? America's atonement could be presented as a weekend of forgiveness, resolve, and purpose to uplift America's honor, with dignity and inspiration to the United States and the world. A national expression of atonement by all government branches and institutions dedicated to expressing hope and courage to the American spirit for the soul of America. Atonement week designed to create remorse for injuries and abuse to arouse the American spirits to radiate hope and desire to make a new the power of forgiveness and hope. The thrust would be to break out in song, dance, and spoken word. The energies and soul of the multicultural spirit through the arts. These creative actions would energize and bless this nation and bring peace to the beautiful souls in this multicultural country.

Many other ethnic Americans like Chinese, Filipino, and Japanese people also suffered persecution and ill-treatment, and abuse historically as well. Personally, I believe that in order to build a movement for atonement for America's abusive and violent practices this nation needs to begin repentance by asking for atonement. Political leaders from official government positions

Sitting in his wheelchair Pope Francis prayed at the cemetery of the former church-run residential school in Maskwacis, Alberta on Monday, July 25, 2022. Pope Francis was offering atonement for the innocent children who perished under the genocidal practices of the missionary-run schools designed to eradicate their indigenous language and culture.

Copyright © Nathan Denette, The Canadian Press via AP

in the executive and legislative branches can begin advocating for a rational nationwide practice for atonement to heal America's wounds in our nation. I strongly believe that a national atonement project can be established for the purpose of atoning for racial and ethnic abuses and killings of innocent ethnic people in America. Historically, this nation has carried the ethnic groups in America: Native American, African American, Asian American, and Mexican American. A commission be established at the national level by the justice department to help organize a system to make it possible to recognize and set up a national day of atonement to honor all victims of such tragedies. This process of atonement when completed can then be sent to our U.S. government to encourage action, forgiveness, and healing for all the victims.

In the 21st century, an atonement message was given by Pope Francis in Canada apologizing for school abuses of genocide by church-run religious facilities. On July 25, 2022, Pope Francis asked the Indigenous people for forgiveness for "The evil committed at church-run facilities." Sitting in his wheelchair Pope Francis prayed at the cemetery of the former church-run residential school in Maskwacis, Alberta on Monday, July 25, 2022. Pope Francis was offering atonement for the innocent children who perished under the genocidal practices of the missionary-run schools designed to eradicate their indigenous language and culture. Many innocent children were abused physically and suffered trauma which led to their deaths. The Canadian government sanctioned their removal from their families and homes and ordered them to attend these missionary schools led by Catholic religious schools. His remarks of apology were first given to Native Indigenous leaders in a pow-wow circle of the Native community where he expressed "Francis added that his remarks were intended for every Native community and person" before his speech Pope Francis visited a cemetary where the local Indigenous community people believe were buried in unmarked graves. He said he was deeply sorry

---

American attitudes and race by Frank Newport, Gallup News conclusive analysis: 1) Blacks in America today continue to report living a life in which they confront bias and discrimination on almost all fronts. 2) Americans are no more positive about race relations today than they were in decades past, and in some instances are. 3) There is a substantial gap between whites and blacks perception of the position of blacks in the U.S. society. As a nation, the racial divides and racial inequalities have intensified within our society. Pew Research Center on April 09, 2019 in a report on *Race in America 2019* by Juliana Menasce Horowitz, Anna Brown, and Kiana Cox indicated that the public has negative views of the country's racial progress. More than half say that Trump has made race relations worse.

- a remark that triggered applauses and approving shouts. He continued that he was deeply sorry for the ways in which many Christians supported the colonizing mentality of the powers that oppressed the Indigenous peoples." I am sorry," he continued, "I ask forgiveness in particular for the ways in which many members of the church and of religious communities cooperated, not least through their indifference, in projects of cultural destruction and forced assimilation promoted by the governments of that time, which culminated in the system of residential schools." - San Diego U-T Tuesday, July 26, 2022 (pps 1 & 8). In the article "Pope in Headdress Stirs Deep Emotion in Indian Country" on July 26, 2022, by the San Diego Union-Tribune, Pope Francis delivers an emotional message of atonement to members of native indigenous members who experienced cultural genocide by missionary members in Canadian schools run by Catholic missionaries. In the article, the Pope apologizes for school abuses. This is a significant and historical statement by The Pope of the Catholic Church whose followers represent over one billion people. As leader and head of the Catholic Church, the Pope is addressing the evil system of cultural genocide conducted in Canadian schools run by Catholic missionaries. Personally, I pray this fact of atonement will lead to deep healing and that Pope Francis' appeal for forgiveness will be accepted by the Native people!

From 13 March 2013 until his death in 2025, Pope Francis was head of the Catholic Church and sovereign of the Vatican City State. On 21 April 2025, Easter Monday, Pope Francis died of a stroke at the age of 88 at Domus Sanctae Marthae in Vatican City.

THE BEAUTY AND POWER OF AMERICAN MULTICULTURALISM IS RENEWING AMERICA

Multiculturalism today in the United States is in the process of a new and vibrant movement of stretching culturally as a nation. As America reaches out, bends, and begins to stretch its cultural body, it finds itself stretching to be an inclusive "we" as Hollinger has expressed the optimistic movement America is experiencing, becoming a united American society. In many cities, towns, urban and rural throughout the nation, the multicultural reality is appearing, growing, and shaping a unique American Identity with social and cultural consciousness.

Multiculturalism is adding new vitality, expansive presence, energy, freshness, and beauty to people's lives in all areas of the American experience and culture. It is transforming daily experiences into a unique reality that is filling cities, towns, villages, and major urban centers. The growing multicultural reality is a fabric of intense color of culture and consciousness and is creating a greater and dynamic fabric called cultural democracy that is ever-changing, resilient and blending the best and resilient of cultures. These beautiful gifts are the rewards that enrich American society and make this country unique and powerful. Multiculturalism is a new, enduring tapestry cloth weaving that enfolds all. The power of American multiculturalism is being blended naturally and is infusing American society with a great multicultural richness, which began in the colonial period. Vibrantly, it is widening and stretching the American Fabric and cultural landscape to a new "we" as Americans. With a national atonement, the people can learn to understand and forgive the past injustices and detrimental abuses of man's cruelty to man and grow stronger as a nation, learning to respect all peoples who have made this country the greatest of nations.

Emerging American multiculturalism can be the new reality for a promising future and for a more accepting, and inclusive American society that lies in the hearts and minds of the majority of Americans for a more inclusive America. These powerful social and cultural dynamic forces are awakening a new consciousness for appreciating differences and similarities as well. Each day, the United States grows in greater recognition and a quiet acceptance of its value as the "We" in America that is being reshaped by the increasing varieties of human ethnic demographies of its people. The American spirit of shaping history and culture in challenging times is a test that has been conquered throughout historical crises especially, like September 11, 2001. On this day, Americans became united as one, truly living in unity with its diversity.

Daily, new social and cultural interactions are experienced through language, media, music, religion, food, art, dance, culture, and politics. The American identity is being stretched and reshaped delicately and sometimes by shoves, gentle pushes, pressures, movements, and interactions emanating from its ethnic communities and from all layers of its vast nation. This happens in all areas of the rural landscape from the urban cities and towns inviting all immigrants to gather from all corners of the world in search of the American Dream in the land of liberty and democracy, where all seek a safe and secure future for themselves and all their families. Everyone can dream to grow together and embrace the new cultural shifts in a healthy and positive nurturing way or react with fear and ignorance and remain in isolation. Each person needs wisdom, strength, and courage to grow and be open to the new multicultural reality and become part of the expanding reality of diversity and nurture this new growing reality of multiculturalism that embraces inclusive democracy that shines our American Light on our identity and become a "Light Unto All The Nations." This shining reality will be expressed in the powerful mediums of art, music, and dance where the beauty and spirit of multiculturalism are celebrated throughout the Land of America.

The immense question facing the U.S., a nation of immigrants, is how can we all become united as "we" as Americans? This question can help determine how to grow and prosper as a nation. Will we find ways to keep ourselves separate and fearful or find a way to live as a diverse nation united by an American Creed that appreciates and integrates all our ethnic and cultural diversity and its beauty and strength? The shocking and horrendous attack on this nation occurred on September 11, 2001, which took thousands of innocent lives and rocked the nation, security, and psychological sense of impenetrability, which people must never forget! After the devastating attack, Americans expressed their dignity when the cartoonist, Conrad, from the *Los Angeles Times* depicted a united identity as Americans as the country faced the tragedy. After facing this devastating threat, the people united completely as Americans and not as hyphenated Americans during the crucial period following the attack. Can we find a way to fulfill the American Creed and embrace cultural diversity, continue greatness, and be a "Light Unto All The Nations," based on a united sense of "we" as Americans? The U.S. must embrace its American cultural diversity with the promise and spirit of the American Creed and revitalize

Multicultural collage of people representing the diverse faces and identities of the American culture in the United States, a nation of immigrants.

Copyright © Canva

a new America to bring about an authentic community shaped by cultural diversity and democracy to radiate throughout the world and bring light and hope for all to see and experience.

AMERICA'S RICH CULTURAL DIVERSITY

The image with the multicultural collage of people is a portrayal of the myriad faces that collectively weave the fabric of American society. It stands as a testament to the United States' unique identity as a nation of immigrants, representing the diverse cultures, backgrounds, experiences and perspectives that have shaped and continue to define the American narrative—diverse, interconnected, vibrant, and resilient.

Conclusion

FULFILLING AMERICA'S PROMISE IN THE TWENTY-FIRST CENTURY

Can we, as Americans in the United States, work toward creating and restructuring a truly authentic, healthy, vibrant, and prosperous multicultural and multiethnic nation for all—one based on a welcoming tolerance that unites all Americans? Can our American culture and spirit be renewed to achieve greatness and wisdom to embrace the emerging cultural democracy of the "we" of America? Can we remain faithful to The American Creed that enshrines and enriches our core American values? As multiculturalism in America adds to strengthen the nation, its foreign policy with its inclusiveness will broaden in scope and balance to seek greater building blocks to further enhance this nation throughout the world. The brilliance of the American Creed endures a positive national increase in its stature and stability to make for an effective and engaging foreign policy for the future in this new century. Multiculturalism will reflect a greater degree of the American spirit unified by all its diverse cultures and united as Americans. As this process of multiculturalism permeates its foreign policy, the spread will strengthen and project a vibrant and inclusive foreign policy for the 21st century. This growth of multiculturalism will benefit America and the world and will bring about a greater American society and a vibrant foreign policy that will contribute to a constructive, and important multilateralism, essential for constructive cooperative foreign relations. This challenging process will become *The New American Revolution*, which will newly unite all Americans in all its diversity and will become the greatest challenge of this new century.

The United States of America, as a divided nation, must find the key formula to unite its nation as a healthy and functioning democracy. As concerned voices of this country, the people must address the great division within and stop selfish, autocratic Extremists like the Trumpers from pursuing dangerous attempts to create another January 6 insurrection and coup in this nation. As a people who love this country, it's critical to find ways to prevent the growing threats and disruption to democracy and extremism perpetuated by false conspiracy theories that discredit the truth and the principles for justice and equality. American citizens have the duty to be engaged and involved in civic projects that build the American Creed for all segments of society. It's important to keep the focus that preserving democracy is the promise, the light, the legacy for justice, and equality for all persons in America. The U.S. country is the possible model of democracy for the world! It has been the beacon of hope and a life where one can survive and follow individual dreams and purpose. Influenced and inspired, the people are called upon to do their best to keep the spirit alive for democracy, for themselves and their families, and for a hopeful and promising America. May each American be a beacon point of light, energizing others with loving kindness, truthfulness, and patient collaboration for the betterment of all life.

The United States national flag proudly waving over the Capitol Hill Building in Washington, DC, stands as an inspiring symbol, capturing the enduring beauty and spirit of the American nation.

Copyright © Canva @rabbit75_cav

Review Questions

QUESTIONS FOR ANALYSIS AND METHODOLOGY

1. **A.** Does multiculturalism in the extreme exist yet in the United States and does it have the possible danger of bringing about detrimental fragmentation in American society? **B.** Define "extreme multiculturalism" and analyze Huntington's thesis.

2. **A.** Does multiculturalism have the potential to subvert American domestic institutions? **B.** Examine educational institutions and political parties.

3. **A.** Do the forces of multiculturalism have the power to negatively impact or weaken multilateralist trade systems and pacts or security concerns that are of interest to the U.S.? **B.** Do cultural ethnic minorities constitute a "fifth column," cadres of latent terrorists, or the leadership of dissident movements?

4. **A.** Is multiculturalism contrary to core values of the American Creed as identified in Huntington's thesis? **B.** Huntington's thesis constitutes an equation in which all factors must be reduced to a lowest common denominator to be solved. Thus, Huntington's abstract concepts must be reduced to practical approaches to multicultural enrichment traits and approaches to determine the potential of immigrants for integration or for maintenance of a separate cultural identity.

5. **A.** Examine nations seeking solutions to multiculturalism. Can the forces of multiculturalism lead to a separatist counter culture that seeks independence? **B.** Canada: Quebec and British Columbia: the responses of government to cultural diversity. **C.** Switzerland: The peaceful coexistence of cultures within a federalist framework. **D.** Japan: The practice of total cultural intolerance.

6. Who coined the term "American Creed," which identifies the American core principles?

7. Why do both Huntington & Ruggie fear ethnic militant multiculturalism? Explain.

8. Identify the core principles or values of the American national identity.

9. List several core fears of Huntington.

10. Ultimately, Huntington recognizes that the American Creed is unlikely to lose its appeal. Explain.

11. What is meant by the term "Creedal Passion?" according to Huntington?

12. Identify the basic concerns of immigrants coming to the United States and their aspirations.

13. Ruggie admits that the "culture wars" have lessened and have become less threatening. Explain. Also explain what he means by culture wars.

14. Describe the positive analysis of Hollinger on the development of multiculturalism in America.

15. Identify the positive findings of a Californian research project on the attitudes of African Americans and Hispanics.

16. What is Dahl's analysis of The Future of Democracy? Discuss the importance and role of the ordinary citizen.

17. Describe the meaning of cultural democracy and multiculturalism for America. How is it related to the core principle of democracy?

THIRD CASE STUDY KEY POINTS

- Plurality and American foreign policy: American values and multicultural trends.

- Brief highlights of immigration to the United States, voluntary and involuntary.

- The growth of American ethnic groups and their political culture: Afro-American, Chicanos-Mexican American, Jewish, Italian, Irish, Midwest, Native American, and Russian.

- American institutions and Americanization of ethnic groups. Civil Rights era and the Cold War.

- Comparative studies of ethnicities in Canada, Switzerland, and Japan.

- The Vietnam War, ethnic revitalization movements and repression:

Black Power Movement, Chicano Movement, and American Indian Movement.

- Demographic changes in U.S. society: The 2020 U.S. Census Bureau has calculated the count of population for the United States to be 331.4 million.

- Multilateralism and multiculturalism: NAFTA's impact.

- Positive and negative aspects of multiculturalism.

- Educational standards and multiculturalism: Backlash against multiculturalism.

- The American Creed versus multiculturalism-an assessment: Challenges of diversity and inclusion.

- Conclusion and evaluation of one or more hypotheses and related questions addressed in study.

THIRD CASE STUDY SUMMARY DEBATE:
PART TWO

"The Pursuit of Happiness," Hope, Joy, and Resilience for All: Embracing and Manifesting Four Cherished Words of the American Creed

BECOMING THE "WE" IN AMERICA AND MANIFESTING THE LIGHT UNTO ALL THE NATIONS TO BECOME THE HOPE OF ALL THE NATIONS AND PROMISE FOR HUMANITY. THE MANY POINTS OF LIGHT ILLUMINATING THE WAY

Questions for Analysis:

1. Can multiculturalism in the extreme threaten the core values of the American Creed and American Foreign Policy? Can multiculturalism alter our basic core beliefs?

2. Can the principles of multiculturalism and a multicultural creed be compatible with our core principles of the American Creed and benefit our national culture, identity, and American foreign policy? Can multiculturalism enrich and give greater value to the American Creed?

RUGGIE STRONGLY ADVOCATES FOR A COMPREHENSIVE FOREIGN POLICY THAT SECURES AND PROTECTS U.S. INTERESTS INTERNATIONALLY

John Gerard Ruggie is a brilliant political theorist and scholar of the highest caliber, and in his excellent work: *Winning the Peace: America and The World Order in the New Era*, he examines America's possible responses and vital concerns in the formation of a stable yet flexible American foreign policy in this new era of the post-Cold War period. As a theorist, Ruggie offers an insightful analysis of America's direction to refocus U.S. policies to establish an enduring peace within the framework of a multilateralist position. According to Ruggie, this critical, refocused multiculturalist perspective will provide a balanced and cohesive approach that will provide greater integration of important aspects of the world economy and security. Ruggie also explores the domestic, cultural, and political forces of concern

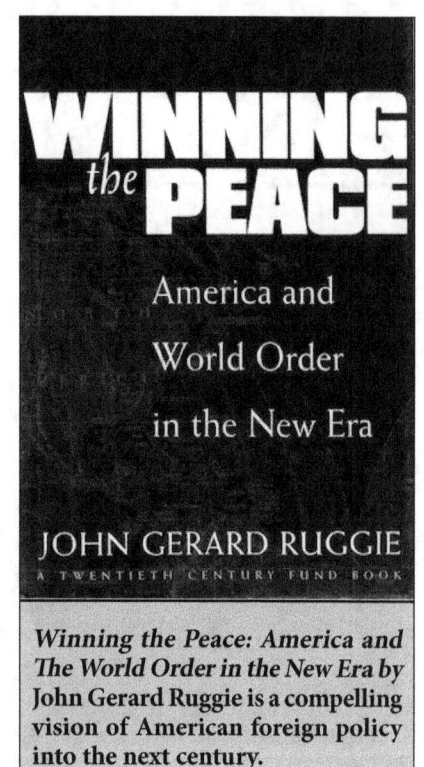

Winning the Peace: America and The World Order in the New Era by John Gerard Ruggie is a compelling vision of American foreign policy into the next century.

within United States society that he thinks are important social considerations, which need to be examined to sustain an effective and comprehensive America. Domestically, he recognizes the importance of America's role and the efficacy of the government in dealing with the nation's pressing problems in the areas of improving health care, education, homelessness, violence, crime, and national defense. Also, relationships, family, safety, genders, environment, networking, literacy, and media communications are areas that need attention in our society of America today.

RUGGIE'S CONCERN THAT CULTURE WARS CREATED EXAGGERATED OPPORTUNISTIC ENTITLEMENTS

Ruggie worries about the source of tensions that he calls the "cultural wars." They began to take shape in the late 1960s in American public life. The source of tension or cultural wars have given "America public discourse and political life since the late 1960s, splintering the ideational project of American community into multiple, competing, and often presumed mutually hostile identities" (Ruggie 167). Ruggie expresses great disdain for the movement and its adherents for being competing identities who challenged the academic canon of the curricula in the humanities and social sciences. "Advocates sought to deconstruct the canon and lay bare the underlying hierarchies based on race, gender, sexuality, as well as other forms of real or imagined domination." Further thoughts on the impact of multiculturalism in America are expressed by Ruggie in which he characterizes self-serving multiculturalism protests negatively as being opportunistic and exaggerated and simply for self-promotion for the new perceived disadvantaged class (Ruggie 167).

"In its place, under the rubric of multiculturalism, they have affirmed the particularism of the exploited, disadvantaged, or merely ignored, at the extreme, the history of diasporas. In the political realm, a parallel movement, which began with the objective of extending the rights of individuals that inhere in the constitution, ended with institutionalized entitlements on behalf of categorical victims" (Ruggie 167).

THE RISE OF ETHNIC NATIONALISM BEGINS TO RESHAPE THE U.S.POLITICAL LANDSCAPE FROM EXCLUSION TO INCLUSION, OPPOSES AMERICAN FOREIGN POLICY ON THE VIETNAM WAR CONFLICT, AND WAGES AN ACADEMIC MOVEMENT TO INTRODUCE ETHNIC STUDIES ON AMERICAN CAMPUSES AND UNIVERSITIES

As a result of the rise of ethnic nationalism of the 1960s and 1970s in America, a severe reaction occurred in a form of a political backlash that Ruggie has termed as neoconservatism, which makes him question and come to terms with the extent of what kind of viable foreign policy can be shaped during this period of "separatist politics." "It is difficult to decipher, what affirmative foreign-policy missions would self-evidently command support within a nation defined by such competing preferences" (Ruggie 167).

Ruggie is correct in affirming the challenge of including multiethnic and multicultural activists and militants in the traditional canon of the humanities and social sciences in the 1960s. A small number of ethnic scholars from elite universities, supportive of this emerging social identity movement, began to assert through their research, and views, criticism of the standards by which the United States academic institutions presented research, theories and views of American ethnicity, principally Negroes (later to adopt the ethnic label as Blacks, and then African Americans) while other ethnicities actively militant were Mexican Americans and American Indians or Native Americans. The main point of contention of the academy was that the canon's perception of these ethnic groups was negative, distorted, and stereotypical. The ethnic construction and model presented and taught at universities perpetuated serious ethnic and cultural misperceptions, and the ethnic scholars believed that it was necessary to provide a more accurate image and understanding of their history and culture that really was undistorted and reflected a more positive view of their experience and contributions as Americans. As Ethnic Studies departments and programs were established after much agitation and demonstration from student activists and supporters, a great influx of politics and "culture wars" brought a high level of polarization among the militant groups, who were in many cases nationalistic and expressed anti-U.S. imperialism during the Vietnam period of conflict and anti-white attitudes. Therefore, it is understandable that Ruggie writes disparagingly of the new militants, for some leaders polarized campuses by their militant actions. However, when social movements arise, the radical levels, in the beginning, usually reach a point after a degree of agitation and intensity and push when the movement reaches a new plateau and comes to achieve an acceptable level of moderation in society. Social pressures ease and adjust to less stress as some degree of understanding and accommodation occurs between militants and established leaders. Then, the balance is reasserted to establish a more cooperative level of understanding. Ruggie expressed concern over this period as he writes "the divided and hostile identities that took shape in our nation" (Ruggie 167).

CIVIL RIGHTS MOVEMENT AND THE COLD WAR, THIRD WORLD AND NATIONALIST POLITICS

Another dimension of the "politics of separation and dissent" on America's university and college campuses in the 1960s was the ideological pressure of the Cold War and the hostility between the United States and the Soviet Union, after World War II. E.J. Hobsbawm, in his work, *Nations and Nationalism Since 1780*, examines the development of nationalist movements in (now referred to as) the "Third World" that emerged from the postcolonial era and were in many cases perceived as leftist movements. At the same time, U.S. policymakers were alarmed about the threat of Communism in the Third World and were steadfast in their policies to contain its spread, especially in the sphere of American influence. More radical student activists and supporters often supported nationalist-liberation causes and their leaders and heroes (Che Guevara and Fidel Castro) of the Third World, who stood up to the powers of imperialism and U.S. might. In the efforts to win the hearts and minds of the nationalists, the propaganda wars accelerated between the United States and the Soviet Union. The Soviet Union challenged the United States about its stature as a democracy and its exercise of "American Democracy" that denied Negroes (later to be self-identities as African Americans), particularly regarding the right to vote, hindered by Jim Crow laws in the South. The leadership of Reverend Dr. Martin Luther King, Jr. introduced a non-violent movement on behalf of civil rights for African Americans, and he would later expand it to represent all poor people. All Americans who were poor and marginalized regardless of their ethnicity were coming to be the focus of Dr. King before his assassination in 1968. He planned to hold a Poor People's March in 1968 in Washington D.C. which occurred over time as the movement continued without him. If it had been successful, his movement could have aroused favorable public opinion, and it had the potential to shift attention from vital foreign policy objectives in military and space development to domestic, economic problems of the poor and perhaps bring about a shift from defense spending to spending in the domestic arena.

At this critical time, it was unknown if the growing tensions and frustration over the United States foreign policy goals over Vietnam War would have enough of an impact to change its policy, but this civil movement to reorient policy to shift to the underclass had the potential to create a divide in society and weaken U.S. leadership in a time of severe crisis during the Vietnam War and the Cold War.

ETHNIC NATIONALIST MOVEMENTS IMPACTED AMERICA'S FOREIGN POLICY ADDED PRESSURES TO END VIETNAM WAR

Ruggie questions and wonders what kind of foreign policy could have been formulated in this divisive political environment. As political changes in civil rights came to the United States through legislative acts, the nation

---

Dr. Martin Luther King, Jr. was shot and mortally wounded on April 4, 1968 in Memphis, Tennessee.

was beginning to face serious ethnic and racial divides (Black Nationalist movement, American Indian movement, Chicano movement) in America, and this activity would show the world through its foreign policy that the United States did have democratic legitimacy and that all its citizens could exercise their civil rights. I think that the Civil Rights Movement and the ethnic nationalist movements through their activism did make a significant impact indirectly on American foreign policy. Civil rights legislation, the 1964 Civil Rights Act and the 1965 Voting Rights Act, were direct consequences of the urban plight of the poor and the inferior social, economic, and educational conditions, as well as discriminatory covenants that gave the Soviet Union political propaganda weapons to use against the United States and U.S. foreign policy. The Civil Rights Movement of the 1960s was part of the generation of which Samuel P. Huntington, a major political theorist of significant influence as a scholar in international relations. He has identified this social and political restructuring in American society as being a "creedal passion" period that has occurred at major points of development in American history in which the American polity and its leaders have sought to narrow the gap between specific liberal values and its institutions that define America's identity and the principle of equality in America. The necessary government action and policy to reduce the gap and bring about equality made up an extremely important mandate for American ethnicities, who were victims of racial discrimination and racial covenants in parts of the U.S. In the post-World War II period, for instance, "for the first time in American history, equality became a major object of governmental policy," and Huntington also adds that "The reformers of the 1960s brought into existence an 'imperial judiciary' in order to eliminate racial segregation and deep inequalities" (Huntington 226). Further, the Vietnam War, which began in the early 1960s and expanded to momentous proportions, absorbed the entire nation and came to reflect a great political divide as the country experienced a national mobilization of many segments of the population, organized to pressure American leaders, particularly President Lyndon Baines Johnson and his administration to end the military conflict in Vietnam and Southeast Asia.

Among those speaking against the conflict were the voices of the ethnic underclass whose fathers and grandfathers and those from past generations valiantly had served with distinction in many wars dating back to the Civil War. A majority of the ethnic youth questioned the war and had serious reservations, for it seemed to them that they, being from the underclass and non-college status, were prime candidates, while their many unnumbered white middle-class counterparts were mostly enrolled in colleges and universities away from the call to arms. With the many white youths or the Anti-War Movement, the ethnic youth leaders began to protest the high attrition rates and casualties that were disproportionate compared to the rest of the American populace. Mexican American servicemen suffered twenty percent attrition rates, and they were twelve percent of the population in the United States. As a group within the anti-war movement, the ethnic revitalization and nationalist movement and their stand against the conflict, united with the creedalists, added to the pressures to end the war. This development had a real bearing on American foreign policy on hold to finally end the war as American policymakers began to see the futility of the military conflict in Southeast Asia. Therefore, the American ethnic nationalists' resistance to the war did have an impact on American foreign policy as they positioned themselves against the U.S. policy on Vietnam, and they contributed to its demise politically as they participated in the anti-war movement across the nation.

According to the 110th Congress, 1st Session concurrent resolution in the House of Representatives on November 9, 2007 titled Hispanic American Heroes Resolution "during the Vietnam War over 80,000 Hispanic Americans served in the United States Armed Forces, over 3,000 Hispanic Americans died in combat, and 16 Hispanic Americans were awarded the Congressional Medal of Honor." Latinos served together with white troops which difficulted exact counts. According to a U.S. Senate resolution from the 115th Congress recognizing the 2017 Hispanic Heritage Month, Hispanic Americans accounted for approximately 5.5% of U.S. military casualties in Vietnam, while they constituted around 4.5% of the U.S. population at that time. The death rate among Mexican-American soldiers was higher compared to their proportional representation in the U.S. population.

BIRTH OF AMERICA'S AMERICAN CREED ITS POWER AND PROMISE, AND CRITICS OF MULTICULTURALISM. GUNNAR MYRDAL IDENTIFIES THE HEART AND SOUL OF AMERICA, THE AMERICAN CREED

At this point, the case study examines the theories of Samuel P. Huntington and also comes back to more comments made by Ruggie concerning the future of multiculturalism to examine if multiculturalism is truly a negative force in dividing American society and identity if it is detrimental to American foreign policy.

Samuel P. Huntington is a world-renowned scholar and theorist in political science and in the field of international relations. Many of his works had a significant impact on the political intellectual landscape, and they are on the cutting edge of brilliant theoretical thinking. The next section of this paper examines the thesis of Huntington that has specific reference to multiculturalism and its challenge to American identity and American foreign policy taken from his chapter "American Ideals versus American Institutions" from G. John Ikenberry's text, entitled *American Foreign Policy*. In the synopsis and introduction of this chapter, Huntington provides an analysis, arguing that an uneasy relationship exists between America's cherished values and its traditional political institutions. These values are derived from its distinct colonial formation of liberalism that was forged in the eighteenth century and manifested after its war of independence from England. The ideals have been labeled "the American Creed" by the famous economist and sociologist scholar Gunnar Myrdal (1944) from his important work on American society and race in America, first published in the 1940s, *An American Dilemma: The Negro Problem and Modern Democracy*. The values that imbue the American Creed and form the core of American national identity are Liberty, Equality, Democracy, and Individualism. These values are the heart and soul of American values and principles that have shaped the political identity, character, and ideology of America since its inception and have left their legacy on American political culture and influence on American foreign policy. The distinctive creed of values is inspirational but because of its normative principles, according to Huntington, the creed also creates a gap between its values and institutions that leads to a "cognitive dissonance" that ensures disharmony in the American political system and American polity-and American foreign policy. Huntington argues that this paradox results in a reaction that manifests itself in two ways, "in attitudes about the institutions that make foreign policy and in attitudes about changing the institutions and policies of other societies to conform with American values" (Huntington 219). In a closer look, Huntington believes that three important possibilities exist that can have a significant impact and influence on the equilibrium of the future of the American Creed that can possibly occur in American society and in turn directly affect American foreign policy. "First, the relation between ideals and institutions could continue unchanged. Second, it could be altered by developments within American society. Third, it could be altered by developments outside American society and by American involvement abroad" (Ikenberry 221).

Further examination of possible changes that could alter the relationship between American political ideals and institutions, and affect the American Creed, which involves changes in American society and the international system as it relates to the ideals and institutions in America, according to Huntington are as follows: "1) **The content of the ideals could change; 2) The scope of the agreement on the ideals could change; and 3) The nature of American political institutions could more closely approximate American ideals, thereby reducing the gap in an illiberal, undemocratic, anti-individualistic direction, or some combination of these developments could take place"** (Ikenberry 221). Historically, twentieth century immigration to the United States introduced a new and different "ethnic" to American culture according to Hofstader (1951), and recent immigration to the United States (from the 1950s to the present) from Latin America, Central America and Mexico could alter the equilibrium of the American Creed, in contrast to the Lockean liberalism that shapes the American identity.

Early 20th-century immigration of Catholics and Jews from central, eastern, and southern Europe profoundly "introduced a new 'ethnic' into American cities," according to Hofstader. In the latter 20th century, the United States experienced its third wave of postindustrial immigration whose immigrants were primarily from Puerto Rico, Mexico, Cuba and others from Central America and Latin America. Huntington believes that like their predecessors, the more recent arrivals possibly "could well introduce into American society political and social values that are markedly in contrast with those of Lockean liberalism. In these circumstances the consensus on this type of liberalism could very likely be either disrupted or diluted" (Huntington 228). New arrivals of immigrants have historically forced America to be the "promised land" and have accepted their "new" country America's values with their heart and soul. Personally, I believe Huntington's view to be without merit.

HUNTINGTON BELIEVES IMMIGRATION TO THE U.S. COULD ALTER AMERICAN CREED VALUES. IS MULTICULTURALISM A THREAT TO AMERICA, AMERICAN IDENTITY, AND AMERICAN FOREIGN POLICY? AS CRITICS BELIEVE?

The focus of this case study is to examine if multiculturalism, as a component of American social and cultural thought and value, is disruptive to the American identity internally and if its influence can create a weakness in domestic and foreign policy. Therefore, the case study examines the two most dominant ethnic groups of the multicultural society in America: African Americans and Latinos (the largest number among the Latino groups are Mexican Americans followed by Puerto Ricans, and people from Central America* and Latin America**) and a related phenomenon that impacts American society-immigration to the United States.

In essence, Huntington speculates that the American Creed could possibly experience a dynamic change from within, which is the second hypothetical premise that he formed in the introduction of his thesis on the American Creed. **Huntington writes that "Latin immigration of the 1950s, 1960s, 1970s could reinforce the central role of the American Creed both as a way of legitimizing claims to political, economic, and social equality and also as the indispensable element in defining national identity" (Ikenberry 229). Huntington also acknowledges that former "children and grandchildren of European immigrants of the early twentieth century became ardent adherents to traditional American middle-class values" (Ikenberry 229). Accordingly Huntington believes that as Americans become more culturally pluralistic, so does the nation as a whole and if cultural pluralism encompasses linguistic pluralism "the more essential the political values of the creed become in defining what it is that Americans have in common" (Ikenberry 229).**

Huntington makes perfect sense concerning the reality of cultural pluralism while recognizing that in identifying cultural and ethnic differences among its vast population, there must also be a common identity in spite of cultural differences, where a social and political agreement that exists brings all the diverse multiple groups, ethnic and non-ethnic, together under the same rubric as Americans. This is a major and uniquely American history and cultural-political process that new immigrants and American ethnic groups have experienced. These ethnic Americans have struggled for equality by seeking to

---

Central America and Latin America are regions encompassing numerous countries with diverse cultures and populations.

* Central America: Belize, Costa Rica, El Salvador, Guatemala, Honduras, Nicaragua, and Panama.
** Latin America includes countries from Mexico in North America down to countries in South America and and some parts of the Caribbean: Argentina, Belize, Bolivia, Brazil, Chile, Colombia, Costa Rica, Cuba, Dominican Republic, Ecuador, El Salvador, Guatemala, Haiti, Honduras, Mexico, Nicaragua, Panama, Paraguay, Peru, Uruguay, and Venezuela. Please note that the list of Latin American countries can vary depending on definitions and contexts, and some territories may be considered dependencies or overseas regions.

overcome racial and social barriers, structural impediments and conventions ingrained in American white culture, and thinking based on racial and social discrimination. These unfortunate systemic discriminatory practices towards them have barred them from receiving their legal rights as citizens, denying them their status of equality as full Americans. The push for fairness, justice, and equality has been undiminished throughout American history and ethnic Americans' movement for equality and acceptance continues to the present day with great urgency. The principle of EQUALITY is an important part of the American Creed, which inspires those to seek it, and becomes part of the human struggle. The quest for equality resonates in the heart of all who seek respect, dignity, and justice.

As Huntington has shown, I personally believe that early twentieth-century European immigrants embraced the American Creed values. Likewise, the immigrants of the twenty-first century also embrace the American Creed values enthusiastically and overwhelmingly and pursue the American dream that America offers. I strongly believe that we as a nation should give full support to aid the group of children who came to the U.S. as children with their parents or whose parents are not U.S. citizens. They are products of American culture, and society and know no other country, but must exist in a limbo state as non-Americans. They all call themselves Dreamers, and they are American-reared and certainly deserve U.S. citizenship.

Huntington in a more critical vein writes, "At some point, traditional American ideals-liberty, equality, individualism, and democracy may lose their appeal and join the ideas of racial inequality, the divine right of kings, and the dictatorship of the proletariat on the ideological scrap heap of history." **While Huntington allows for this possibility he suggests that this is not likely to occur. "There is, however, little to suggest that this will be a twentieth-century happening"** (Ikenberry 229). Because of September 11, 2001, quite fortunately a new sense of unity following the tragic attacks on American soil has stirred the soul to a sense of national oneness as Americans and with cooperative symbolic expression has proclaimed pride in their country and collaboration in being Americans. The people of the United States of America have rallied to its defense to face its enemies and threats to their beloved country and have been victorious and resilient. There is no evidence of immigrants to the U.S. rejecting the American Creed values in the twenty-first century. In reality, the new immigrants to the U.S. embrace the American Creed enthusiastically and overwhelmingly.

Other theoretical considerations that could occur, Huntington speculates, are that the historical identification process of the creed that operates in defining American national identity could over time become "conceivably less significant, and widespread belief in the creed could consequently become less essential to the continued existence of the United States as a nation (Ikenberry 228). If this happening would occur, then the actual American identity would be weakened by creating a lesser need for the ideals to define the American identity for the future. To replace American ideals, the historical, traditional, and cultural customs could possibly add a new sense of a shared experience that could come to define the American identity, according to Huntington. Some or all of these factors generated by social or political pressures can come into play as our society may seek to reduce the gap between these values and the reality of American institutional practice. Nevertheless, Huntington explains, **"Yet the likelihood of this occurring does not seem very high." Even though the American ideals and values have their origins in the seventeenth and eighteenth centuries, they have a "tremendous persistence and resiliency in the twentieth century. The ideals and values have been easily adapted to the needs of successive generations," writes Huntington. In reference to ethnic groups Huntington writes "they have historically reinvoked the ideals to meet their predicaments in their search for equality and in the future they can be expected to reinvigorate those values in order to gain their rights and just rewards in American society" (Ikenberry 228).** Personally, I agree with this view for evidence of greater political involvement in voting practices and civic participation among ethnic Americans and newly naturalized citizens indicates an increase in political affairs that impact their lives.

American institutions and government voter services must continue to build positive outreach services to promote voter education and participation in citizenship outreach. It is important to never forget that this is a nation of immigrants and their contributions have made this nation great. Also, it is important to provide key resources to promote productive outreach for voting, voter education, and American citizenship.

THE OUTBURST OF CREEDAL PASSION ALTERED THE INSTITUTIONS OF THE 1960S AND 1970S TO CONFORM TO THE LIBERAL IDEOLOGY

According to Huntington, the efforts to lessen or reduce the political gap between the ideal-versus-institutions and processes of American foreign relations in American history had led to a direct reduction in the United

States' ability to exercise power in international affairs as well as in its ability to reduce that gap between American values and foreign institutions and its policies. Conversely, Huntington writes, "that efforts to encourage foreign institutions and practices to conform to American ideals require the expansion of American power and thus make it more difficult for American institutions and policies to conform to those ideals" (Ikenberry 233). Quite the opposite results occurred domestically after World War ll. The incompatibility between values and institutions became more acute as the United States was forced to maintain a large-scale institutional central role in foreign affairs and policy. A major development of liberal influences emerged in an "outburst" of creedal passion that occurred in the late 1960s and 1970s, which pressured institutions in foreign policy and security to conform to the strict requirements of liberal ideology.

The targets of the liberal movement were the Central Intelligence Agency, the Federal Bureau of Investigation, the military abroad and the entire military-industrial complex, and the imperial presidency, which Huntington identifies as part of the crusade to tame the large-scale institutions and reign them into more acceptable levels. While the crusade did curb the institutions and brought them into account, it also "seriously, undermined and weakened the power and authority of the government and seriously detracted at times from its ability to compete internationally," according to Huntington.

"The shift was one of the most significant consequences of American involvement in Vietnam, Watergate, and the democratic surge and creedal passion of the 1960s" - Huntington

Huntington's example of the creedal passion of the 1960s and 1970s shows how the power of civic society asserted its voice against American foreign policies, emphasizing they did not agree with or support it. The movement of creedalists based on American idealism was at war at home with American policies that led to corrupt practices and an unpopular war. The gap between American values and its institutions was challenged, as domestically American political interests had to recalibrate their policies to the more acceptable American principles of the American Creed. The new realism of the 1950s and 1960s was challenged by the "new moralists." "The shift was one of the most significant consequences of American involvement in Vietnam, Watergate, and the democratic surge and creedal passion of the 1960s." "The United States is, in reality, the first, most liberal and democratic country in the world with for better-institutionalized protections for the rights of its citizens than any other society" (Ikenberry 240).

This fact is one of the reasons that U.S. policies were changed in order to end the Vietnam War and produced Civil Rights legislation, which eventually passed, restoring and giving rights to the ethnic Americans who struggled for civil rights and justice, which were part of the creedal passion development seeking racial equality for African Americans. This effort to reduce the gap on behalf of disenfranchised and dissenting ethnic Americans to provide civil rights to its ethnic citizens in the post-war period was for instance "the first time in American history, equality became a major object of governmental policy. The reformers of the 1960s brought into existence an 'imperial judiciary' in order to eliminate racial segregation and inequalities" (Ikenberry 226).

The American Creed has "tremendous persistence and resilience" in American Tradition, Identity, and Value For Today and The Future - Huntington

Huntington addresses the possibility that the newest wave of immigrants from Mexico, Central, and South America has the potential to alter drastically the character of the American Creed or to basically reject Lockean liberalism that has shaped this nation. However, he acknowledges that this change most likely will not occur and that the American Creed has **"tremendous persistence and resilience"** in American tradition, identity, and value for today and the future.

The transition of both major ethnic groups, African American and Latino, into American society's mainstream, also indicates a high level of acceptance towards American middle-class attitudes, and values and its elite, and this acceptance also applies to new immigrants. As new immigrants adjust to American culture and society, they will alter their traditional customs and become more accepting of the new culture. Therefore, Ruggie's direct observation of America's ethnic groups and their role in the "culture wars" and Huntington's hypothesis that immigrants will reject the American Creed, in my opinion, are not accurate. Another cultural reality of immigrants is influenced by their socioeconomic status and position on the economic scale. New immigrants are not, in the beginning, centrally involved in any major political processes and policies. They are mostly concerned about their survival in the new country, adjusting to the new language and culture, and establishing economic stability. They mostly are not able to have any effect on the policies that formulate public policy. In most cases, they do not have the time, means, resources, or leisure to do so, for their focus is on economic and social survival. Those who are fortunate and who may gain a better position in the labor force will also be joined by others from diverse backgrounds and countries like Iraq, India, Africa, the Philippines, Caribbean Basin, and Latin America. They may be from multicultural backgrounds, and they have very rich customs and dialects, but they also may not be politically active because of their struggles to survive and their unwillingness to offend the authorities. Studies indicate that new immigrants have strong family and religious values and exhibit conformity to majority norms or aspire to middle-class values in American society.

A recent example of new immigrants coming to America was thousands of Ukrainians seeking refuge in the U.S. The refugees from the war conflict as Russia attacked and invaded Ukraine mercilessly and killed thousands of innocent civilians. An invasion that started on the 24th of February 2022 and as of the point of writing this in March 2023 continues underway.

Therefore, Huntington offers the hypothesis that the new wave of U.S. immigrants could potentially alter the balance of the American Creed but because its strength, vitality, stability, and beliefs are so powerful, this is not likely to occur, he admits. As a theorist, Huntington speculates about this internal possibility but in reality, evidence shows that just the opposite is the norm.

NEW IMMIGRANTS ADHERE TO THE AMERICAN CREED AND EMBRACE HOPE AND PROMISE

While keeping many of their cultural traditions, religions, and family cultural customs, newly naturalized U.S. citizens are overwhelmingly adherents to the sanctity of the American Creed and readily adopt its principles as part of their new American identity. Polls of naturalized citizens indicate a high voting record and a strong identification with the American Creed and the U.S. Constitution.

Newly naturalized Americans reflections on citizenship in a fragile political era by Kale Grumke on August 1, 2019. This report on the voices of newly naturalized U.S. citizens was reported by Judy Woodruff on PBS NewsHour. Here are comments on becoming newly naturalized U.S. citizens from a naturalization ceremony in Alexandria, Virginia:

Edgardo Ramirez from El Salvador. *"It's a very special moment because there's a lot of people that would really like the opportunity to do it, and* *there's just no way they can. I'm glad it's coming to an end, and I don't have to worry about any potential problems from not being a citizen. Today, my wife, Jessica, and my daughter were kind of nervous on the way here because she sees the news sometimes, too. And she asks "Daddy, what are you going to go do today?" And I just told her, you know, I'm just going to become a U.S. citizen, and I don't have to worry about any of the stuff you see on the news."*

Edgardo Ramirez came to the U.S. as a five-year-old child in 2000 and his process to become a U.S. citizen took 16 years. *"I have had a pathway here since I came here because both my parents were here and they were here for a long time. But, you know, there's virtually no pathway for people to come here just because they're trying to get away from violence and, you know, poverty and struggles of their countries. It's not that easy. People who have minor infractions, they don't have a way to become naturalized. And, you know, they have been torn apart from their sons, daughters, wives, and family members here. I just think it's very unfair. I'm just glad that I'm finally a U.S. citizen, after a long wait."*

Sarah Taylor, the District Director in the Washington District of U.S. Citizenship and Immigration Services, welcomed and congratulated a diverse group of newly naturalized citizens. *"Congratulations you're American citizens! At this particular ceremony, there were immigrants from 56 countries!"* The list of countries follows.

Ha Nguyen from Vietnam. *"I am from Vietnam... To be able to vote is something that I think is very powerful, to be able to participate in that democracy. I am excited for November and elections beyond. Earlier in the room, there's a message from the president as well (Trump). Like very welcoming and other things. And it kinda sounded like a script, compared to what he's currently saying out in the news."*

Mattie Hunsaden from the Philippines. *"I'm originally from Philippines, and today I took my oath as a U.S. citizen. This is The Land of Opportunity, so I am really looking forward to what opportunities I can explore in this country."*

Doreena Phoenix. "If you're here in America, you have to obey the laws and follow the laws."

Also, included are the words of John Lee, the father of Lunisa Lee whose women's individual all-around final at the Tokyo Olympics earned her a Gold Medal. Lee's comments are from an article of the San Diego

Union-Tribune written by Juliet Macur on July 30, 2021. **With Biles out Sunisa Lee seizes the moment to capture all-around Gold by Juliet Macur.** *"Sunisa's parents were children when they escaped Laos as their relatives fought on The American side during The Vietnam War. Lee grew up in St. Paul Minnesota populated by Hmong immigrants. As children, they fled to refugee camps in Thailand and from there came to the St. Paul area where 80,000 Hmong live today in 2021."* John Lee's words express his joy and love for his daughter Senisa and his love for the United States. *"People say the United States is The Land of Opportunity, and I am living proof of that,"* John Lee said Thursday in a television interview. *"For my kid, a Hmong girl, to be on the world stage winning a Gold Medal, it's just the best feeling ever."*

Comments such as this and the others listed in this short summary by newly naturalized U.S. citizens, greatly resonate and reflect the deep love and respect for American core principles and luminous qualities of the American Creed. Their love and spirit add life and hope for the vitality and future of America.

A personal comment on the newly naturalized citizens to the United States is by Edgar Olivares who was born in México City. I have known Edgar for forty-three years. He was naturalized on June 25, 2014. He commented to me about becoming a U.S. citizen. *"I have now two mothers, one is México, and the other one now is the United States. The United States has given me the opportunity to help my community. I love the U.S. and respect its values and has allowed me to grow as a person."*

As new immigrants qualify for permanent residency and become naturalized citizens, they are generally required to speak, read and write English at an intermediate level, be of good moral character, and take the Oath of Allegiance in which they promise to defend the Constitution. The fervor of newly naturalized citizens and their respect for their newly found country are contagious, and they have a profound attachment to their new citizenship and the U.S. Constitution. Recent electoral polls indicate that new citizens have a high involvement and participation in voting and take great interest in elections as well as remaining loyal citizens and adhering to the laws of their newly adopted nation.

While new immigrants pursue their lives in employment, family, education, and social development, and they contribute to our system as taxpayers, they add

---

In 2000, the Latino population surpassed the African American population

to the cultural fabric of this country. Therefore, I agree with Huntington that the new wave of immigrants does not pose a threat to the beliefs and principles of the American Creed, but is drawn to its promise, hope, and possible fulfillment of it. The idealism of the American Creed based on its fundamental principles speaks universally to the world of a better life of hope and promise that does not exist anywhere else. **The present and/or past generations of immigrants have not sought to refashion the American Creed but have embraced it and have sought to make it even more of a reality.**

RUGGIE SEES COMMON GROUND IN "CULTURE WARS"

Ruggie notes how the United States government has changed and grown significantly in the last fifty years since World War II and how the role of the United States has expanded in protecting its international security, economic interests, and relations in the economic global system. He believes that the fundamental sense of American identity has been weakened as the result of "unresolved tensions" within American society and will likely impact domestic opinion and any future U.S. policy. Briefly, his concerns revolve around, first, the expansion and centralization of the federal government. He believes that it is natural for a scaling back of the government to occur to diminish the dominance of government over individual states. To do this reduction will require a political contestation period among leaders and most likely foreign policy will become secondary to the domestic agenda. Second, the electoral alignment that began when George Wallace's election (1968) caused a split among the Southern voters and impacted foreign policy since historically the South had supported Roosevelt's internationalist agenda and foreign policy and the new political impulse of the Republican party had been more inward-oriented and less aggressive on government regulations on trade policies (Ruggie 1996).

The third issue is what Ruggie calls the "culture wars" which concern him for the splintering of the American community, which is harmful as it creates divided and competing, mutually hostile, identities. He is very sensitive in attempting to assess what kind of foreign policy can emerge from such a splintered community faced with such different needs and orientations. "It is difficult to decipher what affirmative foreign policy missions would self-evidently command support within a nation defined by such competing preferences" (Ruggie 168).

Although Ruggie has expressed concern over the "culture wars," he is somewhat reassured that cultural conflicts have lessened and become less threatening to American domestic relations in the United States. "It is somewhat reassuring then, to recall that these cultural conflicts are not nearly as severe as earlier ones in this century have been. In addition, there are also theoretical reasons and survey data to suggest that considerably more common ground exists than has been supposed in these debates" (Ruggie 167).

As mentioned, there has been a lessening of the ethnic revitalization movement through the historical period of the 1960s and 1970s. The ethnic group leaders exercised their militant strategies of marches, sit-ins, rallies, and political demonstrations. As a result, they gave their input into the political system; thus, their needs were articulated and aggregated, creating new political space in the political arena.

Today, major ethnic groups, organizations, and leaders are serving as political representatives in local and state assemblies and in Congress. As their leaders become more involved at the decision-making levels of leadership, they are not guided solely on ethnic and cultural platforms or agendas but also on ideology as politicians who serve a constituency of both ethnic and non-ethnic members in the community. The politics of confrontation have passed to the standard politics of accommodation, where domestic and international interests become central to their leadership as political leaders with special interests relate to the constituents to ensure that maximum equality is being served to all.

FINDING COMMON GROUND

As mentioned, Ruggie acknowledges that there may exist more common ground than was thought (Ruggie 167). According to influential historian David Hollinger from the University of California at Berkeley who is an analyst of multiculturalism and its movement, he sees signs that multiculturalism is creating more positive interaction toward a more harmonious relationship in American society. He "sees hope that this debate is circling back in search of new means for a 'stretching of a we'" (Ruggie 168).

Although Hollinger sees that "pluralism does not suffice as a common ground because it endows with privilege particular groups, especially the communities that are well-established at whatever time the ideal pluralism is invoked" (Ruggie 168). Personally, I partly agree with Hollinger in his view that the invocation of pluralism does grant some degree of benefit on behalf of the pluralists when the ideal is invoked. However, achieving a common ground for the pluralists historically has been the challenge, and that is why they invoke a certain benefit on their behalf because the social and political conventions have been undemocratic and have denied them their constitutional rights of equality and historically, the vote (Voting Rights Act 1965), which is the center of American citizenship.

As members of civil society, ethnic Americans play an important role in rectifying imbalances that prevent them from exercising their rights as citizens. Their political dissent, protected by the Bill of Rights (the First Amendment) is embedded in American tradition, and the lack of unanimity is an acceptable kind of discourse that reflects a healthy political culture and a civic society in pursuit of democracy. Their activism or dissent, their disagreement if expressed and exercised within the laws, contributes to the ongoing development of democracy in American society and is commendable in my view. If domestic relations of all Americans, especially ethnic minority groups were harmonious and the debate on equality was fulfilled, even among ethnic Americans, greater solidarity with domestic policies would most likely overlap with American foreign policy matters to a greater degree. The tensions of "culture wars" as identified by Ruggie would diminish.

During The Vietnam War, the practice of "fragging" was a serious problem among Army soldiers who threw hand grenades to eliminate the Army officers, mostly white and some black soldiers fragged their white officers. This unfortunate practice appeared on the battlefield within the U.S. armed services while fighting against the enemy. Within this act lay the core of racial tension and anger and frustration on a racial level between black and white America. This behavior was an example of how deep and complex race relations in America have been and how it erupted and spilled onto the battlefield.

Hollinger proposes that instead of ancestral heritage or culture, American society should look to the future and not to the past and make the social construction of citizenship the common civic character. "In the civic character of the American nation-state he insists, in a nationality (that is) based on the principle of consent and is ostensibly open to persons of a variety of ethnic racial affiliations, a civic nation built and sustained by people who honor a common future more than a common past" (Ruggie 168).

If ethnic Americans were to accept Hollinger's and Ruggie's position to deny the distinct past, everyone would suffer an identity loss of major significance. In addition, ethnic Americans, in the process of accommodation to civic characters and institutions, would weaken the hard fought-sacrifices gained and would disrespect the valiant struggles of self-determination and justice that many generations have suffered and died for. Ethnic Americans must remain steadfast to preserve the historical and cultural past at all costs.

OUR HISTORICAL PAST SHOULD NEVER BE FORGOTTEN

Personally, I strongly disagree with Hollinger and Ruggie's views on the past. The past should never be forgotten. The past very importantly is connected to, shapes the present, and impacts the future. It is of great importance to preserve our historical memory of our past for all future generations. However, I do agree with Hollinger's position that civic character is a definitive force of fundamental importance for America and can perhaps in time develop as a unified whole for the nation. Hollinger makes an excellent observation in constructing American citizenship on our common civic character and not on ancestral heritage or social identity construction. This view, however, eliminates the cultural history and identity of new American citizens, who make cultural uniqueness richer. As Americans, I strongly believe we have the power and determination to adopt the American civic character of this nation-state as declared by Hollinger and supported by Ruggie. Maintaining proudly the heritage and culture of its ethnic identity and relishing both of these realities as Americans, we can live fully and nurture all of these unique values with distinction and honor.

Robert Putnam, a renowned political theorist, bases his research on civil society. He identifies the role and importance of civic trust and participation, and he affirms that these vital ingredients are important to the principles of democracy and democratization. Further Putnam's essay, "Bowling Alone: America's Declining Social Capital" is an insightful look at the importance and role of public life and society's performance as its social institutions are influenced by the norms and networks of civic engagement and contribute to democracy and the process of democratization. He notes and affirms that a severe decline in civic trust and civic-mindedness was the result of the tumultuous period of the 1960s and 1970s arising from the social and political cleavages of Watergate, Vietnam, and the Civil Rights Movement (Putnam).

SIGNS OF ETHNIC REVITALIZATION MATURING AND THE AMERICAN CREED'S ADAPTABILITY AND RESILIENCE OF HOPE AND PROMISE OF OUR TIME

The rise of ethnic revitalization movements moved through this conflictual period and has become more accommodational and less militant. Today in America, a new engagement in which American ethnics are pursuing civic and social justice in all realms of life to better their social, economic, educational, and political lives in accordance with American principles of democracy. Their greater movement indicates a growing civic character and identity that are beneficial and positive and lend to Hollinger's view of building a civic nation that can be transformed to a greater level of a civic nation with a civic character encompassing its citizens.

Interestingly, Ruggie tells of a California research project that analyzed the attitudes of Blacks and Hispanics who responded to questions dealing with immigration, language, cultural identity maintenance, multiculturalism, and foreign policy. In general, they both scored high on multiculturalism and found in regard to foreign policy, "The researchers conclude on bases of available data that the core - what they call 'Cosmopolitan Liberal' - American sense of identity remains a relative bedrock that could provide support for diverse foreign policy positions, especially "instrumental" though not "ideological" support for multiculturalism'"(Ruggie 169).

Ruggie's sense of concern should be eased as the respondents have a strong attachment to the Lockean principles of the American Creed and support the general American foreign policies that constitute American interests. The report concludes that the American sense of self-participation remains relatively intact. They indicate more interest in political ideals of egalitarianism, as well as a fundamental sense of America's role in the arena of international relations, but appear to remain more focused on the domestic interests that relate to their social and economic livelihoods, such as employment, education, immigration, crime, and violence issues that directly impact them and their families. This focus may explain their lack of ideological support for multiculturalism and greater interest in their social needs based on domestic concerns.

LATINOS BECOME THE LARGEST ETHNIC GROUP IN AMERICA IN 2000

As the American ethnics have continued to increase in population, particularly the Latino groups, and as the result of high birth rates and immigration, the Latino population since 2000 is now the dominant ethnic group, replacing the African American group who formerly was numerically the largest group in terms of their population. They are becoming more crucial to the dominant political parties in the United States.

Ethnic Americans are dominating in terms of numbers in major cities and critical states such as New York, California, Florida, and Texas. The leadership of the Democratic and Republican parties in order to exercise a stable and unified American foreign policy will need to garner votes from these constituents, and this need will require a friendly and nurturing kind of strategy that speaks to their issues to win their support. California's Proposition 187 (1994) spelled the rise and fall of former California Governor Pete Wilson, a Republican, who effectively used the anti-immigration fervor to rekindle his political career but fell short in the presidential race and never acknowledged how their hard work and contributions added to the economy in a positive way which helped promote a thriving California economy for the state and nations.

Proposition 187, which passed in November 1994 in California, was politically an expedient and hot button issued by then Governor Pete Wilson, the thirty-eighth governor of California from 1991 to 1999. However, fortunately, it was declared by the federal court judge that it violated the United States Constitution and also issued an injunction to bar its implementation. Governor of California, Pete Wilson failed in his attempt to attack the undocumented worker failed. Governor Wilson scapegoated the undocumented Mexican immigrant, which caused racial divisiveness and prejudice toward a vulnerable social group doing manual labor, agricultural work, and other low-paying work for construction and building areas of employment. Proposition 187 was an attack on hard-working people who labored at low wages to earn money for themselves, their families, and also for families living in Mexico. Proposition 187 in California demoralized them and caused psychological harm to a vulnerable group living in California without proper documentation. The hard facts revealed that these disciplined hard workers, through their paychecks, paid taxes and never received any benefit due to their illegal status. Their work and contributions through their labor were never recognized or respected.

The Mexican undocumented worker was severely exploited by Proposition 187 for political gain by the political aspirations of Governor Wilson who was seeking the U.S. presidency. Fortunately, Governor Wilson's ambitions and political plans never materialized. The after-effect of Proposition 187 was a "political earthquake" among the Mexican workers who were in a position, after years of living in a state of limbo, of not naturalizing to become U.S. citizens. Proposition 187 shook them to their core to be proactive and seek naturalization to become U.S. citizens.

Proposition 187 in 1994 was responsible for creating California's "political earthquake" after its passage. Subsequently, the expected number of permanent residents applying to become citizens to protect their rights and improve their status was projected to be upwards of 300,000 new citizens. These new citizens are mostly registering as Democrats, and this statistic is a wake-up call for Republicans who traditionally have been characteristically uninterested and a hindrance in developing political space for American Latinos and most other Democrats, African Americans, and other non-whites. President George W. Bush's leadership should be credited for casting General Colin Powell as Secretary of State and Condoleezza Rice as National Security Advisor, both African Americans included in important decision-making positions.

MULTICULTURALISM THREAT DIMINISH

Ruggie expresses questions concerning the uncertainties surrounding foreign policy as the end of the Cold War has produced a state of political fluidity that has created party realignments and an unpredictable electoral base which affects the support or lack of support for an internationalist agenda. Based on his book in which he proposes his theories for a multilateralist framework, his concern over the cultural tensions appears to be appeased, based on recent research that he has encountered, which shows that the multiculturalism threat has diminished.

American Identity and Immigration to the United States

In the 1750s, Benjamin Franklin created a cartoon called "Join or Die." It was a response to the debate about unity among the colonies during the French and Indian War. According to Moser and Watters, colonials portrayed their American identity as anglo men to unify a common defense strategy during this conflict (Moser and Watters). Also in the eighteenth century an observer, Hector St. John de Crevecoeur who came from France, was taken aback by the diversity of the inhabitants and settlers new to America. He writes "a mixture of English, Scotch, Irish, French, Dutch, Germans and Swedes this promiscuous breed." And questioned, "what then is the American, this new man?" And he answered, "Here individuals of all nations are melted into a new race of men" (Schlesinger 129).

Alexis de Tocqueville in his famous observations of America in his book called *Democracy in America, emerging* in the mid-1830s and in other writings on American democracy, observed that the origin of American identity was that of Anglo-Americans, and while they differed greatly from each other on different principles, they all shared a common feature and that was language. The language was the common bond that united them and enabled them to communicate and understand their common concerns (Moser and Watters). America became

J O I N, or D I E.

Benjamin Franklin's warning to the British colonies in America "join or die" exhorting them to unite against the French and the Natives, shows a segmented snake, "S.C., N.C., V., M., P., N.J., N.Y., [and] N.E."

Copyright © Franklin, Benjamin. "Join or Die." Illustration. The Pennsylvania Gazette, May 9, 1754. From Library of Congress Prints and Photographs Online Catalog. http://loc.gov/pictures/item/2002695523/ (accessed January 10, 2006).

more diverse in the eighteenth century: for example, Jews and Catholics were fleeing religious persecution, and Italians, Swedes, Chinese, and Russians seeking opportunities were incorporated and assimilated into the American identity.

In the 1840s, Irish immigrants came to America to escape Ireland's Great Potato Famine. At this time Germans outnumbered the Irish and constituted the largest ethnic group in the Census of 1870. Then Norwegians came and surpassed the Irish in number. The Germans heavily populated the Midwest, referred to as the "German Triangle." At the tum of the century, new immigrants from Italy, Greece, and Eastern Europe joined the urban center of New York, the second largest city in the world, numbering four million. These new residents challenged the Germans, Irish, and Scandinavians in terms of a numerical advantage in the United States.

Arthur Schlesinger, Jr., in his article, *Cult of Ethnicity,* warns how today the new ethnics are obstructing the past assimilation and integration of American identity, which implies that it could impact domestic solidarity and create instability in leadership in American foreign policy. He comments that today throughout the world there exist great ethnic tensions that threaten the nations of the world. "On every side, today ethnicity is breaking up nations. The Soviet Union, India, Yugoslavia, and Ethiopia are all in crisis. Ethnic tensions disturb and divide Sri Lanka, Burma, Indonesia, Iraq, Cyprus, Nigeria, Angola, Lebanon, Guyana, Trinidad - you name it. Even nations as stable and civilized as Britain, and France, Belgium and Spain face growing ethnic troubles. Is there any large multiethnic state that can be made to work?" (Schlesinger 129).

Schlesinger, Jr.'s comments on assimilation, however, are not entirely accurate. To begin with, the earlier immigration movements in the eighteenth and nineteenth centuries are quite different from the immigration waves of the 1960s to the present. There are numerous developments in communication, technology, and modes of transportation that allow newer immigrants to keep in closer contact with families back home. In the past keeping a link to their native lands was extremely difficult and made assimilation and integration much more likely. Even so, many of these groups lived in their self-styled neighborhoods and ghettos. The newer immigrants from Latin America and ethnic citizens (African American and Latino) have adjusted to show their allegiance to the United States, have fought in wars for the United States, and have had to organize and lobby to be included and integrated into the United States society to overcome racial and discriminating policies of "separate but equal" institutions.

The Movement for Inclusion, Ethnic Tensions, and Societal Differences

This movement of inclusion has not been to separate from America and cause fragmentation of identity but has sought to be a part of American democracy and society, to be treated like all other American citizens (Garcia). The observation Schlesinger, Jr. makes concerning the ethnic tensions and flare-ups in the regions do exist and create internal problems. However, this observation is more complex. The breakup of the Soviet Union was not the result of ethnic tensions but of political disintegration from within. It is impacted by history, culture, and politics to very distinct societies and I think it is not applicable to the United States. The United States is a First World country, and the other regions the author alludes to are Third World countries. Tensions are part of everyday life and are impacted by the forces of modernization and urbanization, it is likely that the tensions under discussion are unique to the United States. As witnessed in Yugoslavia, ethnic rivalries and tensions can be used for political purposes to unify people in the form of nationalism in order to gain territory and political power. Yugoslavian leadership at the top effectively used the concept of "ethnic cleansing" to get rid of non-Serbian elements in order to consolidate more territory for the Serbian regime. Ethnic tensions will always exist, and so to apply the problems of other regions generically and then conclude that these same tensions exist in the United States is not the best way of understanding the nature of these tensions. The ethnic tensions of other regions of the world are rooted in different social, economic, and political, historical realities.

In E. J. Hobsbawm *Nations and Nationalism*, the author traces the meaning of nations and nationalism since 1780 and comments that only after 1880 in the United States did it begin to matter to the ordinary individual to think about nationality. It then became important for politicians to know more about how the ordinary man and woman of the pre-industrial age understood and felt about nationality so that they then could build a nationalistic spirit. He comments, "Ethnicity has no historic relation to what is the crux of the modem nation, namely the formation of the nation-state" (Hobsbawm 64). He writes that ethnicity has served mainly as visible markers highlighting differences to reinforce distinctions between "us" and "them," therefore, skin color has played a major role in setting groups apart into separate social positions. He says "ethnic differences have played a rather small part in the genesis of modem nationalism" (Hobsbawm 67).

While the Spanish conquered numerous indigenous groups in the New World and imposed a caste system that separated the population into racial castes, Hobsbawm finds no evidence of a nationalist movement. He also believes "no single African state, not even Ghana and Senegal, whose founders were inspired by Pan-African ideas, have developed a nationalist movement." Historically, nationalism gained ground from the 1870s to 1914 because of urbanized societies, migrations, and the pace of change and friction among groups. Nationalism reemerged from mobilization from the lower middle class of the counter-revolution of fascism. Nationalism associated with the left grew during the anti-fascist period and was reinforced by the anti-imperial struggle in former colonial countries. The wave of nationalism that once swept the world has since declined, according to Hobsbawm, which began after World War II. In the United States, three prominent groups were part of the nationalistic movement. One was the Black Panther Party, which was militant and believed in armed struggle. The American Indian Movement was also militant and believed in armed struggle. The third group among the Chicano generation was radical, but not revolutionary, according to political scientist scholar, Mario Barrera from UC Berkeley. The Brown Berets were a paramilitary group, militant, but never carried out armed struggle in the United States (Barrera).

In the work *The Politics of Power* by Katznelson and Kesselman, the authors mention that observers describe "the increasing fragmentation and conflict within American society, identified as the process of 'Balkanization' or 'atomization'" (Katznelson and Kesselman 106), but mention that the threat to fragmentation of American identity was not jeopardized. "For example, during the entire period, no major movement or political party challenged in a sustained way the basic legitimacy of American economic and political arrangements. Furthermore, although social movements like the women's movement, black militants, and environmental activists achieved significant changes, American corporate capitalism remained intact" (Katznelson and Kesselman 106).

An interesting facet of the Chicano experience during WWll was the influence of sinarquismo (anarchism) from Mexico. This was an extreme right-wing political philosophy with connections to Spain and Germany that emphasized Mexican nationalism and opposition to both Mexican and United States involvement in the War with the Axis powers. This group was active in the urban centers of Los Angeles and El Paso and attempted to dissuade Mexican Americans from actively supporting the war through military service, and also preached the return of the Southwest back to Mexico (Meier and Ribera).

Not until the 1970s did another radical group appear to sound the theme of the return of the Southwest the group called the "August Twenty-Ninth Movement" which sought to create a multinational vanguard role to organize workers to carry on a revolutionary struggle in the United States. The ATM sought to follow the teachings of Mao Tse Tung (sometimes spelled as Mao Zedong). This radical group promoted self-determination among Chicanos and others. They believed that any group was free to determine its own boundaries and could freely secede from the state.

AZTLÁN THE ANCESTRAL HOMELAND OF THE CHICANO MOVEMENT PERIOD OF THE 1960S AND THE 1970S

The ATM held the belief that Chicanos were oppressed and had the right to secede. They, however, did not promote or advocate this action (Barrera). The Chicano generation of activists adopted the historical origin of the Aztecs called "Aztlán," the birthplace of the Aztec people who migrated to the central area of present-day Mexico City in the twelfth century. In the 1960s, Aztlán became the Southwest lands that were lost in the war with the United States and had now become in their ideology, Aztlán of the Chicano generation. Aztlán, the Southwest homeland of the Chicano generation became mainly a symbolic interpretation with no real plan of secession or any other movement to establish a separate union.

However, the discussion of Aztlán was taken seriously by then Secretary of State, Henry A. Kissinger, who was aware of the separatist movement in Canada by French separatists. His concern was noted in a *Time Magazine* article dealing with the adoption of the new Aztlán interpretation that was taking place in the Southwest.

Influential artist and writer, Rudolfo Anaya, of the Chicano generation writes of an *Aztlán Without Boundaries* that takes the Chicano vision beyond a geographical area to a universal level that encompasses an international perspective of cultural and political relations where their rights will be respected. The Chicano leaders adopted the concept of Aztlán as a symbolic homeland, for there never existed an ideology to seek secession. The ideology of Aztlán was to develop self-determination and to promote social, educational, and civil rights.

What is Multiculturalism in America?

THE DRAMATIC SHIFT OF THE 21ST CENTURY OF THE *E PLURIBUS UNUM* TO THE MULTICULTURAL *E PLURIBUS UNUM* IN AMERICA

The debate on multiculturalism or diversity in America is a historical reality and reflects another "cognitive dissonance" as it positions two distinct concepts: one proclaims diversity is our strength and posits the opposite concept that proclaims diversity is the undoing of our core values and identity as Americans. A robust debate on multiculturalism in America is consistent as an underlying pressure that exists and surfaces periodically the social life in America.

Multiculturalism is an attitude of consciousness that recognizes ethnic, cultural, and linguistic differences in American citizens; the mantram of multiculturalism is synonymous with cultural diversity and an emphasis on variety among America's ethnic groups. The mantram promotes tolerance and acceptance of these ethnic and cultural customs and the traditions that make these groups unique.

The anti-multiculturalists, upholding a traditional Americanist perspective of Americanization, hold that this special attention on cultural and linguistic differences among groups separates and divides the unity as Americans. Multiculturalism weakens the country's identity and common bond as it challenges *E Pluribus Unum* (out of the many comes one), it's harmful and undermines the nation. They ask the question of whether the U.S. will become fragmented domestically and weaken its national leadership in international affairs and American foreign policy. The unifying force of American oneness and the will to fight against tyranny and King George of England during the American Revolution 1765-1783. Today, as the country continues to draw many of the world's population, it is imperative to foster a unique oneness to be inclusive for the common good of this nation. Processing the common good and the spirit of *E Pluribus Unum* for a new American diversity that is broadening and accepting among everyone's unique talents and gifts which makes us strong and whole as a nation.

This restorative and accepting *E Pluribus Unum* needs to be incorporated with the American Creed and American vision. *E Pluribus Unum will need to be nurtured and respected and must be added to the American heritage and embraced in the light of American history and diverse legacy based on a legacy of acceptance and respect of all distinct ethnicities and culturally different peoples of the world.* The roots of this legacy and destiny are unique as Americans are living in this unique moment and recreating the renewed fabric of a new America, which enfolds all cultures and ethnicities. All renewal is resting securely in the rich American diversity embracing the American Creed and its principles of equality, liberty, democracy, and individualism. The foundational history and culture of Americans have evolved to become a multicultural and ethnically diverse part of the American fabric which in today's world is a multicultural *E Pluribus Unum*.

Americans face universal challenges impacting health and survival as a nation, and only by being united and whole can the people meet the serious challenges facing Americans and the world. It is important to maintain individual uniqueness as a nation and be totally united as a progressive and constructive force for humanity and a world leader to continue to provide social, economic, and political assistance for other nations in need.

A major reform in American education arose after the 1960s when a multiethnic and multicultural curriculum was incorporated into education to respond to the needs of students and society. In a preamble of educators dedicated to multicultural education, the following principles are found which shape a multicultural creed for educators. The United States forced with serious internal division and polarization can be renewed with generosity and respect for all if we choose and rest securely.

The preamble to NCATE's (National Council for Accreditation of Teacher Education) New Standard

Multicultural education is preparation for the social, political, and economic realities that individuals experience in culturally diverse and complex human encounters. These realities have national and international dimensions.

This preparation provides a process by which an individual develops competencies for perceiving, believing, evaluating, and behaving in differential cultural settings. Thus, multicultural education is viewed as an intervention

and an ongoing assessment process to help institutions and individuals become more responsive to the human condition, individual cultural integrity, and cultural pluralism in society.

- Language and Policy Curriculum

New Philosophy of Cultural Democracy

A Positive Vision for America

AN INNOVATIVE PERSPECTIVE AND EDUCATIONAL FRAMEWORK ENHANCING AMERICA'S VALUE AND VISION OF CULTURAL DIVERSITY FOR THE 21ST CENTURY

Multiculturalism as a discipline and philosophy of education has added another perspective to viewing America. It is a newer educational model or extension that is dedicated to the cultural, ethnic, and linguistic realities of diversity that exist and is called the philosophy of cultural democracy. Multiculturalist advocates based their thoughts on four tenets that frame the mission of cultural democracy:

1. *To create a democratic learning, communicating, and working environment in which individuals respect and celebrate one another's dignity.*

2. *To learn to question and reject present exclusion status among people and broaden an ethnocentric view of our culture.*

3. *To adopt a comparative approach and examine relationships among social groups (based on region, class, ethnicity, culture, religion, arts, and gender) within a framework of democratic ideology.*

4. *To emphasize a sense of community and recognize similarities and differences among a nation of nations.*

(Romo and Salerno 2-3).

LARGE-SCALE DEMOCRACY IN THE TWENTY-FIRST CENTURY

Robert A. Dahl's work, *Democracy, and its Critics* identifies two major political transformations. The first was in the fifth century B.C.E. and the second was in the seventeenth century. The third transformation, according to Dahl, will be in the twenty-first century where the change from a guardianship model of government to large-scale citizenship participation in decision-making processes (Dahl 117). This makes reference to Dahl's Theory on the third transformation of Democracy in the twenty-first century as a point of emphasis and understanding of this critical theory on democracy.

Community-inspired civic participation and citizenship at all levels will contribute to bridging the gap between American ideals and institutions and the influence political leaders and informed citizens in a cultural democratic environment in the twenty-first century (Romo and Salerno). Ordinary citizens will play a greater role according to Dahl's hypothesis and will be empowered in the post-industrial period toward cultural democracy supported by the organizational shifts that will be influenced by the following shifts, according to Romo and Salerno (Romo and Salerno).

1. **From dominance to partnership**
2. **From departmentalization to intersection**
3. **From segregation to pluralism**
4. **From exclusion to cultural democracy**

The cultural democracy model formulated from a multicultural ideology will focus on empowering all citizens to greater participate in a democratic environment. If Dahl's hypothesis comes to be realized, the political system would be broadened, and greater input from society would allow more input in American foreign policy as well. The politically provocative practices of voter suppression and unfair, partisan gerrymandering contribute to the creation of unjust political voting districts. Additionally, the political environment is buffeted by waves of dangerous misinformation, further adding to and exacerbating disruptive practices within the political system and society, resulting in discord and confusion.

Ronald Takaki, a multiculturalist theorist from UC Berkeley, sees California's multiethnic society as a role model for the future as California represents where America is headed in the twenty-first century (Takaki).

If Dahl's hypothesis is likely or becomes a reality where civic participation in society would involve the civic sectors of the middle and lower segments of society, then American foreign policy would reflect a broader section of American society and would represent a fundamental change from the elite to the broader base sectors of American society. This shift would lessen the gap between the ideals and institutions, and greater equality would evolve. Dahl does not speculate on the condition that would create a third wave of democracy in the world in this literature. It is too premature to hypothesize on this development, however, it is hoped that such a shift would allow the United States to protect its interests and security and would not undermine the stability and ideology of its creed (Dahl).

PROTECT THE AMERICAN DEMOCRATIC POLITICAL SYSTEM

In safeguarding the democratic political system, it is imperative for elected political leaders and institutions to remain vigilant and proactive. They must undertake rigorous efforts to monitor and identify any corrupt or harmful anti-democratic practices that may compromise the integrity of the electoral process. Preserving the sacred practice of voting is crucial to ensure the legitimacy of such democratic exercises and uphold the rights of all U.S. citizens eligible to vote.

Especially in these times of heightened political polarization and rampant misinformation prevalent in the U.S. today, the responsibility to protect the democratic values becomes even more critical. By fostering transparency, implementing robust monitoring mechanisms, and combating misinformation, leaders can fortify the foundations of the democratic system. It is through such concerted efforts that a political environment where the voices of all citizens are heard can be sustained, and the democratic principles that underpin the nation are preserved for generations to come.

Canada and Switzerland and Their Ethnic Communities

TWO POSITIVE EXAMPLES OF POLITICAL ACCOMMODATION

While the main focus has been primarily on American ethnic groups, African American and Latino groups, it is key to offer a view of the two nations in their relations and policies towards ethnic groups. The status of ethnic communities in Canada is an important subject of study. The fate of Canada rests on how the federal government will win over the aggrieved French-speaking communities of Ottawa and Quebec and build tolerance for many new ethnic immigrant groups from Asia, West Indies, East Africa, and the Middle East. Historically, the differences between English-speaking and French-speaking communities have been shaped by oppressive institutions that have subjugated French Canadians. The movements to separate from Canada have not succeeded but problems remain, especially in the lack of economic integration among the French speakers in Ottawa. After WWII and after the increase of ethnic groups in Canada, new forms of racial intolerance began to appear among white English-speaking Canadians. Also, the Native peoples-the Indians suffering from exploitation and severe poverty conditions and land issues organized the First Nations Movement. Like the United States American Indian Movement (A.I.M.), they became more militant and staged a standoff over a construction site threatening their sacred land. Their protest was successful. This still continues to be worked out by the government according to Kellas. Canada's source of conflict according to Kellas is not entirely over ethnic or linguistic differences but more because of economic issues that impact the ethnic groups and also the lack of territorial integration (Kellas).

Switzerland offers another interesting case. Switzerland is a leader in the world for building a stable social system and political rule for diverse populations under the banner of mutual inclusivity, acceptance, and tolerance. Based on Morris-Hale's work, *Switzerland: A Paradigm*, he shows how

Switzerland successfully has integrated four different language groups, German, French, Italian, and Romansh, and two religious traditions, Protestantism and Catholicism, in order to form an effective central government and a system of cantons under the system of democracy. The test of its democratic survival is based on its historical longevity, going back to 1291 when a loose confederation was formed into a federation to protect itself from the Hapsburg Dynasty. Switzerland is a small nation with few resources and productive people who developed over generations a stable and cohesive system that integrated its people and was able to resolve internal differences primarily through referendums making ethnic extremism very rare. The citizens are very active in government and law-making. Only in the area of women's suffrage were they slow to accept. In 1971, the Swiss voted to grant women the right to vote. The last holdout was the canton called Appenzell Inner-Rhodes, which finally adopted women's suffrage in 1990 (Morris-Hale).

Ethnic Contributions of Jewish, Chinese, and Japanese

The United States has numerous ethnic groups of significant interest and richness that contribute to the U.S. greatly including Asian and Jewish groups who are influential in this country. Asians have greatly contributed to the development of the United States for over 150 years. The Japanese and Chinese came to America to seek better opportunities for a better life. They sacrificed and labored in America's development in spite of negative racial persecution. In World War ll, the Japanese suffered the unjust internment of 110,000 Japanese Americans, and yet thousands of young Japanese American men proved their loyalty and enlisted in the United States Army (Romo and Salerno).

Jews have been a part of American society since 1677 when they established roots in Newport, Rhode Island. After the nineteenth-century religious persecution of Jews in Russia, many fled to the United States. Jews have also migrated to all parts of the world including South America, Central America, Eastern Europe, South Africa, and Israel. In the 1920s, elite American universities such as Harvard established quotas for Jewish students (Romo and Salerno). They contributed to the Civil Rights Movement in the 1960s participating in the 1964 "Freedom Summer." Unfortunately, they still suffer racial persecution today.

The Jewish diaspora is made up of a large diversity of Jewish groups throughout the world. One major group is called the *Sephardic Jews* who come from Spain and the *Dutch Jews* from the Netherlands. Portugal and Brazil also there is a Jewish diaspora called the *Ashkenazi Jews* of Russia, Poland, and *German Jews* from Germany. In general, the Jewish diaspora is a migration of Jews out of their ancestral homeland to resettle in other parts of the world.

Conclusion

In conclusion, this research reveals the possibility that among the American Creed principles, particularly at this time in history, it is the principle of equality that speaks to the social and political needs of a nation, especially among African Americans and Latinos and other significant ethnic American groups. The cultural democracy or multicultural creed also speaks of the importance of equality of opportunity for all. Therefore, they are mutually the same in this respect. Except that multiculturalists include respect for ethnic and linguistic differences. Fortified with this philosophy, ethnic and social tensions will continue to exist especially among conservatives, but if cultural democracy is strengthened, the domestic and international interests will also be integrated and grounded, and the institutions and policies will reflect greater equality, which will bring benefit to the international arena of life and in American foreign policy.

Personally, I believe we as Americans need to celebrate our rich, social, and cultural diversity and do all we can to move towards unity and inclusivity as we are reminded that we are all from the same source; we all originate in Divinity, which is the loving Heart of God. These inspirational thoughts we must strive to bring about on our American Journey of Democracy in the twenty-first century. The future of our country resides in our hearts and homes. **As quoted in the Bible from Mathew 19:26, "With God all things are possible."**

In the city of Al-Andaluz in Spain, after 700 years (711-1492) Jews, Christian, and Muslims lived creatively, and peacefully coexisting together.

Works Cited

Barrera, M. *Beyond Aztlán*. Notre Dame: University of Notre Dame Press, 1988.

Dahl, Robert. *Democracy and Its Critics*. New Haven, Connecticut: Yale University Press, 1991.

Ferraro, V. "Multiculturalism: A Policy Response to Diversity." *Global Diversity Conference, Resources for the Study of International Relations*, 1995.

Garcia, I. M. *Chicanismo*. Tucson: University of Arizona Press, 1997.

Hayes-Bautista, Dr. D. E. *The Burden of Support*. Stanford: Stanford University Press, 1988.

Hobsbawm, E. J. *Nations and Nationalism Since 1780*. Cambridge, U.K.: Cambridge University Press, 1990.

Hofstadter, R. *The American Political Tradition*. New York: Alfred A. Knopf, 1951.

Hollinger, D. A. *Postethnic America: Beyond Multiculturalism*. New York: Basic, 1994.

Huntington, S.P. "American Ideals Versus American Institutions." *In American Foreign Policy, ed.* 1982.

Ikenberry, G.J. *American Foreign Policy: Theoretical Essays*, 221-254. New York: Addison-Wesley, 1999.

Katznelson, I., and M. Kesselman. *The Politics of Power*. San Diego: Harcourt Brace Jovanovich, 1975.

Kellas, J. G. *The Politics of Nationalism and Ethnicity*. New York: St. Martin's Press, 1998.

Lazarz, Robert. "Diversity is Not our Strength." (Letters to the Editor) *The Telescope*, vol. 55, no. 11, 10 Dec. 2001.

Little, Becky. "Why Lincoln House Divided Speech was So Important." *History Factual Entertainment Brand*, 15 June, 2018, www.History.com

McDougall, Walter A. "America and the World at the Dawn of a New Century." Presented at *Foreign Policy Research Institute*, November 1999. American Diplomacy speech. Philadelphia.

Meier, M.S., and F. Ribera. *Mexican Americans/American Mexicans*. Canada: Hill and Wang, 1993.

Morris-Hale, W. 1996. *Conflict and Harmony in Multi-Ethnic Societies*. New York: Peter Lang.

Moser, J. and A. Watter. *Creating America*. New Jersey: Prentice Hall, 1999.

Nagle, John D. *Introduction to Comparative Politics*. Chicago: Nelson Hall Publishers, 1992.

Pole, J.R. *The Pursuit of Equality in American History*. Berkeley: University of Berkeley Press, 1978.

Putnam Robert D. "Bowling Alone: America's Declining Social Capital." *Latin American Politics Seminar,* Fall 2001.

Reitz, J.R. and R. Breton. *The Illusion of Difference: Realities of Ethnicity in Canada and The United States*. Ottawa: C.D. Hower Institute, 1994.

Romo, J. J. and C. Salerno. *Toward Cultural Democracy: The Journey from Knowledge to Action in Diverse Classrooms*. Boston: Houghton Mifflin, 2000.

Ruggie, J. G. *Winning the Peace*. New York: Columbia Press, 1996.

San Diego State University, Language and Policies Studies Department. *Multicultural Methods and Curriculum PLC 651*, Spring 1988.

Schermerhorn, R. *Comparative Ethnic Relations: A Framework for Theory and Research*. New York: Random House, 1970.

Schlesinger, A.M. T*he Disuniting of America: Reflections on a Multicultural Society*. New York: Norton, 1992.

Seizaburo, S. "The Clash of Civilizations: A View from Japan." *Asia Pacific Review,* Oct. 1997.

Takaki, R. *A Different Mirror*. New York: Little Brown, 1993.

Valdez, John E. 2001. *Multiculturalism in America & American Foreign Policy: Element of Unification or Fragmentation*. Independent Studies Project (Thesis), Masters Program of International Relations, University San Diego, Fall 2001.

Third Case Study Review

REVIEW QUESTIONS ON MULTICULTURALISM IN AMERICA AND AMERICAN FOREIGN POLICY

1. How are the fears and concerns of extreme multiculturalism a credible reality as both Ruggie and Huntington postulate? Give examples of their views on the threats from multiculturalism.

2. Do they believe that their fears on multiculturalism will be likely to occur? Explain.

3. Identify the focal core principles of the American Creed and their meaning underlining the social and political fabric of American democracy.

4. According to Huntington, how can the power of creedal passion create political instability and negatively impact American foreign policy. Discuss the question in the context of the anti-Vietnam War.

5. Identify the lives, concerns, and conformity of New American immigrants who have become naturalized citizens and their relationship to the American Creed.

6. Do you believe that the possibility and likelihood that immigration from Mexico, Central and South American will alter and diminish the core principles of the American Creed according to Huntington? Why or why not?

7. Identify how multiculturalism can contribute positively to America and American society as discussed by Hollinger.

8. Discuss the new engagement of American ethnic groups: African American and Latino in seeking civil and social justice in the democratic spirit of the American Creed.

9. What is the potential and future of democracy outlined by the eminent and distinguished democracy theorist, Robert Dahl.

10. What is meant by cultural democracy? How can it contribute to American society and American foreign policy?

THREE CASE STUDIES

A New Multicultural *E Pluribus Unum* in America and an Inspiration to The World.

John E. Valdez

Three Case Studies Review

The first case study provides the reader with an account of America's Revolution from England and the formation of the American Creed's core principles: liberty, democracy, equality, and rugged individualism. The second case study discusses these dissident movements of the 20th-century a) China: Tiananmen Square b) Mexico: Tlatelolco Square, Plaza of the Three Cultures c) United States: The anti-Vietnam War Movement. The third case study discusses the emergence of America's multiculturalism and its growing influence and contributions to becoming "A light into the nations" for America and the world.

AMERICA'S DEMOCRACY IN PERIL OF BEING THREATENED BY WHITE EXTREMISM

Currently democracy in America, unfortunately, is greatly threatened by growing American violent white extremism. January 6, 2021 insurrection, the attack on the American citadel of democracy, where the U.S. Capitol was terrorized by the mob of Trump domestic extremists. The attack on the U.S. capitol was promulgated by former president Donald J. Trump to disrupt the official certification of the 2019 presidential election declaring candidate Joe Biden as the official winner. Former president Trump has continuously promoted the false idea that the presidential election of 2019 was stolen but has no evidence supporting this false claim. This extremism attack on the nation's capitol has been shocking and disgraceful to the nation. It is a higher level of terrorism when these acts are misguided by those in power, who see themselves above the law, but how can we deal with these leaders when they are already in power?

The nation and the American democracy are in peril! President Joe Biden and Vice President Kamala Harris recognized the bravery and courage of the police to fight off the terrible assault on the sacred steps and halls of the Capitol on January 6, 2021. The U.S. government was protected by the heroic capitol police and the Washington Metropolitan police, who later was awarded the Gold Medal for their heroic actions and efforts to save the Capitol from the radical Trump extremists. Even though this event is over, many believe that another attack against the government can be expected to happen again.

In current times, American citizens see daily signs of divisions throughout the land. I personally sense and feel the deep troubled waters of division and harsh rhetoric in the public sphere of social media news and various other media channels on the national networks. Recalling the famous words of Abraham Lincoln on slavery and its expansion in the 1850s while he campaigned and delivered a speech at the Republican State Convention. Drawn from the words of Jesus Christ in The New Testament Gospels of the Bible, Lincoln eloquently spoke the famous lines "A house divided against itself cannot stand. I believe this government cannot endure, permanently half-slave and half-free. I do not expect the Union to be dissolved—I do not expect the house to fall—but I do expect it will cease to be divided. It will become all one thing or all the other."

How do we bridge the divide? How do we overcome the negative walls of anger and discord to reach consensus and mutual respect as Americans? How can we heal the great disharmony that keeps the two political parties apart and many times unable to work together? Americans must recognize the common good and faith to hold tight to the principles of the American Creed that encompass the history, culture, and common purpose of a nation. Americans have proved that a historical road has been traveled together. As the attack suffered from 9/11 which killed thousands, the people of this country proved to be resilient, proud, and united as Americans stand together.

Personally, I believe that the main dangers now are within our government, in ourselves, and in our hardhearted ignorance as we learn how to view our world more expansively, unselfishly, and more inclusively with respect and reverence for all life. Our outer conditions can change as we live our peace with empathy, forgiveness, and compassionate love, and by living for a way and a creed that is larger than ourselves acting with justice, caring, and generosity of spirit. How can we heal the racial intolerance and the great disharmony and division that keeps the two parties polarized and apart? A plan to bring about reconciliation when we as a nation will be open to working together and let our national priorities be for a restart and a new vision for unification is being inspired by the principles of the American Creed to guide us to a better place as Americans. We are all one in the heart of our creator. Once we are consciously on the path of national reconciliation, we can create a new vision of cooperation, collaboration, and purpose. We strive to generate a rebirth in the hearts and minds and rededicate ourselves in the spirit of our love for our country and its hope and promise based on the American Creed principles: Liberty, Democracy, Equality, and Rugged Individualism. We must strive to be faithful to the "We The People."

As the famous sage Lao Tzu eloquently and wisely commented, thousands of years ago, "The journey of a thousand miles begins with a single step."

Let us take the first step of our journey together.

Let us overcome our fears.

Let us be strong and valiant to face the future with hope and with the Grace of God!

Let us assert courageously *E Pluribus Unum* through the land of America.

Let us stand together for the good of our nation!

Famous activist of the Chicano Movement epic and stirring poem "I am Joaquin" by Rudolfo "Corky" Gonzalez (June 18, 1928 - April 12, 2005) ends with the stirring words

> *La Raza!*
> *Méjicano!*
> *Español!*
> *Latino!*
> *Hispano!*
> *Chicano!*
> *or whatever I call myself,*
> *I look the same*
> *I feel the same*
> *I cry*
> *and*
> *sing the same.*
>
> *I am the masses of my people and*
> *I refuse to be absorbed.*
> *I am Joaquín.*
> *The odds are great*
> *but my spirit is strong,*
> *my faith unbreakable,*
> *my blood is pure.*

I am Aztec prince and Christian Christ.
I SHALL ENDURE!
I WILL ENDURE!

Conclusion

There is a great and colossal concern over the growing and deepening division in the United States of America that is seriously threatening this country's democracy. To end the final chapter, there is a report from Southern Poverty Law Center (SPLC) and a speech from President Joe Biden as he decides to quit the race for the new election year in 2024.

First, here is the *SPLC Report* of Summer 2022 Volume 52 Number 2 published by the Southern Poverty Law Center, 400 Washington Avenue Montgomery, Alabama, AL 36104.

The SPLC identifies 733 hate groups and issues recommendations for protecting democracy.

Democracy at a crossroad

"Our nation stands at a dangerous crossroad," said Susan Corke director of the SPLC's Intelligence Project, which produced the report.

The mainstreaming of hate and extremism threatens our people, our communities, our educational system, and democracy itself.

Fighting back against hate

The SPLC Report provides a wide range of policy recommendations for politicians and individuals that are designed to defend and strengthen the nation's democratic institutions and build community resilience.

The recommendations include speaking out against hate, racism, extremism, and attacks on voting and democratic institutions;

Protecting every citizen's right to vote;

Enforcing current federal and state laws against private militias and political institutions;

Holding the planners and perpetrators of the Jan. 6 attack - and those who inspired their violent acts - accountable, with real consequences;

Improving government coordination and response to domestic extremism;

Confronting white supremacy and extremism among active-duty military personnel and veterans;

Funding hate crime prevention, digital literacy, and anti-bias education initiatives to steer individuals away from hate and end extremism;

Making tech and social media companies more accountable and transparent to promote online safety.

"Pushing back against rising authoritarianism will require a holistic approach," Corke said. "It is urgent that policymakers act to defend and strengthen our democratic institutions, and commit to long-term, meaningful initiatives to counter racism, antigovernment extremism, and hate groups in America."

In 2024, President Joe Biden addressed the nation with an iconic speech in defense of democracy as he shared his decision to quit the race for the new election year. Here is the speech as shared by The Association Press (AP):

President Biden's 7/24/2024 Oval Office Speech

Updated 7:28 PM PDT, July 24, 2024

WASHINGTON (AP) — Transcript of President Joe Biden's address to the nation on July 24, 2024:

*My fellow Americans, I'm speaking to you tonight from behind the Resolute Desk in the Oval Office. In this sacred space, I'm surrounded by portraits of extraordinary American presidents. Thomas Jefferson wrote the immortal words that guide this nation. George Washington, who showed us **presidents are not kings.** Abraham Lincoln, who implored us*

President Joe Biden addresses the nation from the Oval Office of the White House in Washington, Wed., July 24, 2024, about his decision to drop his Democratic reelection bid.

to reject malice. Franklin Roosevelt, who inspired us to reject fear.

I revere this office, but I love my country more.

It's been the honor of my life to serve as your president. But in the defense of democracy, which is at stake, I think it's more important than any title.

I draw strength and I find joy in working for the American people, but this sacred task of perfecting our union is not about me. It's about you, your families, your futures. It's about we the people, and we can never forget that. And I never have.

I've made it clear that I believe America is at an inflection point, one of those rare moments in history when the decisions we make now will determine our fate of our nation and the world for decades to come.

Black lawmakers are standing by Biden at a crucial moment. But some express concern. Biden delivers solemn call to defend democracy as he lays out his reasons for quitting race.

America is going to have to choose between moving forward or backward, between hope and hate, between unity and division. We have to decide, do we still believe in honesty, decency, respect, freedom, justice and democracy? In this moment, we can see those we disagree with not as enemies, but as fellow Americans. Can we do that? Does character in public life still matter?

I believe you know the answer to these questions because I know you, the American people, and I know this, we are a great nation because we are a good people.

When you elected me to this office, I promised to always level with you, to tell you the truth. And the truth, the sacred cause of this country, is larger than any one of us, and those of us who cherish that cause cherish it so much, a cause of American democracy itself must unite to protect it.

You know, in recent weeks it's become clear to me that I needed to unite my party in this critical endeavor. I believe my record as president, my leadership in the world, my vision for America's future all merited a second term, but nothing, nothing can come in the way of saving our democracy, and that includes personal ambition.

So I've decided the best way forward is to pass the torch to a new generation. That's the best way to unite our nation. I know there is a time and a place for long years of experience in public life, but there's also a time and a place for new voices, fresh voices, yes, younger voices, and that time and place is now.

Over the next six months, I'll be focused on doing my job as president. That means I'll continue to lower costs for hard-working families, grow our economy. I'll keep defending our personal freedoms and our civil rights, from the right to vote to the right to choose. I'll keep calling out hate and extremism, make it clear there is no place, no place in America for political violence or any violence ever, period. I'm going to keep speaking out to protect our kids from gun violence, our planet from climate crisis, is the existential threat.

And I will keep fighting for my for my cancer moonshot, so we can end cancer as we know it because we can do it. And I'm going to call for Supreme Court reform because this is critical to our democracy, Supreme Court reform. You know, I will keep working to ensure America remains strong and secure and the leader of the free world.

I'm the first president in this century to report to the American people that the United States is not at war anywhere in the world. We'll keep rallying a coalition of proud nations to stop Putin from taking over Ukraine and doing more damage. We'll keep NATO stronger, and I'll make it more powerful and more united than at any time in all of our history. I'll keep doing the same for allies in the Pacific.

You know, when I came to office, the conventional wisdom was that China would inevitably surpass the United States. That's not the case anymore. And I'm going to keep working to end the war in Gaza, bring home all the hostages and bring peace and security to the Middle East and end this war.

We're also working around the clock to bring home Americans being unjustly detained all around the world. You know, we've come so far since my inauguration. On that day, I told you as I stood in that winter — we stood in a winter of peril and a winter of possibilities, peril and possibilities. We were in the grip of the worst pandemic in the century, the worst economic crisis since the Great Depression, the worst attack on our democracy since the Civil War, but we came together as Americans, and we got through it. We emerged stronger, more prosperous and more secure.

Today, we have the strongest economy in the world, creating nearly 16 million new jobs — a record. Wages are up, inflation continues to come down, the racial wealth gap is the lowest it's been in 20 years. We're literally rebuilding our entire nation, urban, suburban, rural and tribal communities. Manufacturing has come back to America.

We're leading the world again in chips and science and innovation. We finally beat Big Pharma after all these years, to lower the cost of prescription drugs for seniors, and I'm going to keep fighting to make sure we lower the cost for everyone, not just seniors.

More people have health care today in America than ever before. And I signed one of the most significant laws helping millions of veterans and their families who were exposed to toxic materials. You know, the most significant climate law ever, ever in the history of the world, the first major gun safety law in 30 years. And today, violent crime rate is at a 50-year low.

We're also securing our border. Border crossings are lower today than when the previous administration left office. And I've kept my commitment to appoint the first Black woman to the Supreme Court of the United States of America. I also kept my commitment to have an administration that looks like America and be a president for all Americans.

That's what I've done. I ran for president four years ago because I believed, and still do, that the soul of America was at stake. The very nature of who we are was at stake and that's still the case. America is an idea, an idea stronger than any army, bigger than any ocean, more powerful than any dictator or tyrant.

It's the most powerful idea in the history of the world. That idea is that we hold these truths to be self-evident. We're all created equal, endowed by our creator with certain inalienable rights, life, liberty, pursuit of happiness. We've never fully lived up to it, to this sacred idea, but we've never walked away from it either and I do not believe the American people will walk away from it now.

In just a few months, the American people will choose the course of America's future. I made my choice. I made my views known. I would like to thank our great Vice President Kamala Harris. She's experienced, she's tough, she's capable. She's been an incredible partner to me and a leader for our country. Now the choice is up to you, the American people.

When you make that choice, remember the words of Benjamin Franklin. It's hanging on my wall here in the Oval Office, alongside the bust of Dr.

King and Rosa Parks and Cesar Chavez. When Ben Franklin was asked as he emerged from the convention going on, whether the founders have given America a monarchy or republic, Franklin's response was "a republic, if you can keep it." A republic if you can keep it. Whether we keep our republic is now in your hands.

My fellow Americans, it's been the privilege of my life to serve this nation for over 50 years. Nowhere else on earth could a kid with a stutter from modest beginnings in Scranton, Pennsylvania, and Claymont, Delaware, one day sit behind the Resolute Desk in the Oval Office as President of the United States, but here I am. That's what's so special about America.

We are a nation of promise and possibilities, of dreamers and doers, of ordinary Americans doing extraordinary things. I've given my heart and my soul to our nation, like so many others. I've been blessed a million times in return with the love and support of the American people. I hope you have some idea how grateful I am to all of you.

The great thing about America is here kings and dictators do not rule, the people do. History is in your hands. The power is in your hands. The idea of America lies in your hands. We just have to keep faith, keep the faith and remember who we are. We're the United States of America and there's simply nothing, nothing beyond our capacity when we do it together.

So let's act together, preserve our democracy. God bless you all and may God protect our troops. Thank you.

This concludes the final chapter. Every citizen and member of this great nation must find a way to support and participate in these initiatives to save democracy and follow the call to become apostles of democracy for this nation and the world. It is up to each one of us!

About the Author

JOHN E. VALDEZ

Professor Emeritus, John E. Valdez, has taught Chicano in the United States History, Chicano in the United States Political System, and Chicano Literature in the Multicultural Studies Department for 43 years at Palomar Community College in San Marcos, California. He was Chair for 30 years and advisor to the student organization called MEChA throughout his career at Palomar College. John earned three Master's degree 1) Master's Equivalency in Comparative Literature from the University of California San Diego, La Jolla, CA 2) Master's degree from San Diego State University in Language and Policy Studies and 3) Master's degree from the University of San Diego in International Relations.

John E. Valdez

Photo. Published April 20, 2014 by Monica Dattage. The Telescope.

In 2017, he began the Archival Preservation Project dedicated to preserving all relevant educational documents from his archives by donating them to San Diego State University's Special Collections. All archival documents of M.E.Ch.A de Palomar student history and all educational and relevant materials of the Multicultural Studies Department from Palomar College formed in 1974.

As member of the Oxford Roundtable from 2006 to 2009, he has presented papers on Multiculturalism in America and American Foreign Policy, the oral history of the Mexican American pioneer community from the Mexican Revolution to World War II in Lemon Grove, California, and Cesar Chavez' life and his fight for social justice.

Professor Valdez is currently working on a documentary highlighting the first successful desegregation court case in the United States, which was won in March 1931 in Lemon Grove, California. He is capturing the experiences of the pioneering Mexican and Mexican-American community of Lemon Grove, who took legal action against the Lemon Grove School Trustees. The trustees had segregated Mexican American children and intended to send them to a separate school within the Mexican American neighborhood of Lemon Grove. Their legal challenge proved successful, marking the nation's inaugural desegregation victory in March 1931. Professor Valdez includes the Lemon Grove experience, his life growing up in Lemon Grove, and his path of seeking an education. Lemon Grove Oral History Project interviews Mexican American pioneers who settled in Lemon Grove, and sued Lemon Grove School Board in 1931 to stop racial segregation. A special tribute to honor Lemon Grove residents fighting for educational equality for their children. The parents of the Lemon Grove segregated children did not have great social economic status or influence, however, they were aware of the value and importance of education, and wanted their children to be educated and have a better life, economically, as citizens in American society. March 2011 marked the 80th anniversary of the first successful desegregation case in the U.S., the Lemon Grove Court Case. Also, Professor Valdez is planning a photo exhibit of the Valdez family from Mexico during the Mexican Revolution from 1910 to 1929 and family photos of settling in Lemon Grove in the early 1920s.

In 2000, Professor John Valdez introduced the idea of a mural project for the Multicultural Studies Department home room in the Student Union Building SU-17 at Palomar College, San Marcos, California. The mural was named "Adelante MEChA Adelante" by John to capture the sea of students in protest for justice. When the new Multicultural building opened, the mural was placed in the new home room MD-328 where it resides today. The mural features retired faculty from left to right: Anthony Guerra, Jose Rangel, Dr. Luz Garzon and John E. Valdez (mural project on next page).

John is inspired by his son Joaquín (Kino), daughter Mica, daughter-in-law Jessica, and his three grandchildren Julian (12 years old), Jordin (9 years old), and Jayden (5 years old), and all his loved relatives including nephews, grandniece, great great grandnieces, and cousins Maria Luisa Padilla (101 years old) and Judy Smith (103 years old). Maria Luisa and Judy's heroic lives of love and courage inspire our lives to be filled with hope and joy.

They are all John's shining inspiration of Love anf Light!

Adelande MEChA Adelante, Mural Project. This first part of the mural features retired faculty from left to right: Anthony Guerra and Jose Rangel.

Palomar College, San Marcos, California.

Adelande MEChA Adelante, Mural Project. This second part of the mural features retired faculty from left to right: Dr. Luz E. Garzon and John Valdez. Palomar College MECha student leaders from left to right: Ruben Ochoa on left holding casket, Sean O'shea on right holding a casket, and Diana Ortiz on the right side holding her Palomar College degree. Today, Ruben Ochoa is an influential and prominent muralist, and Diana Ortiz is a full time professor in American Indian Studies at Palomar College.

Palomar College, San Marcos, California.

Unfortunately, political division, polarization, and threats to democracy will likely persist throughout the United States. However, there is hope in the enduring strength of the nation's 240 years of institutions, laws, and Constitution to withstand and overcome the difficult and challenging realities it faces.